Fearless and Free to BE

A Faith-Based Approach to Intimate Partner Violence in the African American Community

Culturally Competent Instructor's Manual
& Group Curriculum for IPV

SARAH A. GBADEBO, M.S.

Faith-Based Learning Publications, Inc.

This publication is designed to provide accurate and authoritative information in regard to the subject matter covered. It is sold with the understanding that the publisher is not engaged in rendering psychological, legal, or other professional services. If expert assistance is needed, the services of a competent professional should be sought.

Copyright © 2014 by Sarah Adedoyin Gbadebo

Faith-Based Learning Publications, Inc

41457 51st Street West,

Quartz Hill, CA 93536

www.faithbasedlearning.org

All rights reserved. No part of this book may be reproduced or transmitted in any form by any means, electronic or mechanical, including photocopying, recording, or by any information storage and retrieval system, without the written permission of the Publisher. Excerpts may be printed in connection with published reviews in periodicals without expressed permission.

Manufactured in the United States of America.

Cover design by Lefether D. Jackson

ISBN 978-0-615-96587-1

TABLE OF CONTENTS

Acknowledgment ii

Background iii

Introduction 1

Session 1 Overview of Fearless and Free to BE Group Curriculum 3

Session 2 Shattering the Cycle: Deconstructing the Dynamics of Abuse 10

Session 3 Understanding, Elevating & Equipping the Survivor 13

Session 4 Understanding, Dismantling & Disempowering the Abuser 15

Session 5 Fragmentation of the Family in Violence: Impact of Abuse in the Home 17

Session 6 Living Fearless and Free: Celebrating Your Journey to Freedom 19

Appendix A: Handouts for Fearless and Free to BE Group Sessions 21

References & Further Readings 104

Resources 113

Acknowledgments

First and foremost, I thank the God whom I serve. Were it not for my Heavenly Father and His preordained purpose for my life, this endeavor would not have been possible. I would also like to thank my family and friends for their encouragement throughout the course of my academic and professional endeavors. I extend my deepest appreciation to my parents, Michael Gbadebo and Julia Fortune.

Background

Intimate partner violence is an epidemic within the African American community. Data from the National Violence Women Survey suggest that 30% of African American females are victimized by IPV in their lifetime (2000). While IPV is not an issue confined to one specific cultural group, research suggests that black women report significantly higher rates of IPV than other cultural groups (Black, Basile, Breiding, Smith, Walters, Merrick, Chen & Stevens, 2011). Findings reveal that black women experience IPV at a rate 35% higher than their European American counterparts of comparable socioeconomic status, and 2.5 times the rate of other cultural groups (Bureau of Justice Statistics, 2001). Not only are black women disproportionately affected by IPV, but they are more likely to sustain serious and lethal injuries (Watlington & Murphy, 2006). Consequently, IPV is among the leading causes of death for black women, and has been ranked the number one health issue among African American women (Campbell, Sharps, Gary, Campbell & Lopez, 2002).

With the negative effects of diminished physical health, mental health problems and poor healthcare behaviors as a result of IPV (Lee, Thompson, Mechanic, 2003), there is a dire need for a culturally appropriate intervention to address this community crisis. The availability of general interventions and access to protective resources is not lacking and therefore cannot be identified as the problem for the epidemic of DV in the Black community. Many interventions are available to assist African American IPV victims, including DV shelters, various approaches and orientations of therapy, comprehensive social services, and much more; however, the problem lies in the lack of culturally appropriate services and interventions for this particular demographic.

The use of religion and spirituality have been found to be the most consistent coping strategy used by African Americans to navigate society and daily life stressors (Mattis, 2002; Woods, Antoni, Ironson & Kling, 1999). Religious institutions have occupied a significant position in the lives of African Americans (Watlington & Murphy, 2006), particularly among African American women, who tend to be socialized into the Black church at a younger age than African American men, more likely to rely on their spirituality and religiosity to cope with obstacles (Watlington & Murphy, 2006).

Moreover, data from quantitative studies have documented links between spirituality and faith-based practices and both coping and psychological well-being among African American survivors (El-Khoury, Dutton, Goodman, Engel, Belamaric & Murphy, 2004; Watlington & Murphy, 2006). Findings reveal high levels of spirituality and religious involvement to be associated with less depression and higher religious involvement to be associated with reduction of post-traumatic stress disorder symptoms, also supporting the helpfulness of spirituality and religious practices to African American survivors' well-being. Another study found spiritual well-being among African American survivors to be a protective factor against suicide attempts (Meadows, Kaslow, Thompson & Jurkovic, 2005).

This high cultural reliance on spiritualism and religious involvement evident in the research indicates the centrality of religious involvement and spirituality within the African American cultural experience. Consequently, the use of addressing issues in the African American community through avenues of culturally influential religious institutions, such as the Black church, and tending to faith based components of cultural identity in mental health, is an approach particularly critical for African American women, who tend to rely on religious and spiritual means of assistance more so than traditional mental health services (Watlington & Murphy, 2006). Given the centrality of religious involvement and spirituality within the African American cultural experience, and the historical role the Black church has played in tending to the needs of this community, faith-based institutions have significant potential to serve as a protective factor against IPV.

While the Black church has traditionally served as a pillar of strength, and a source of healing for the African American community, IPV has not always been regarded as a significant issue within the faith community. Often times, misuse of spiritual and religious teachings would serve to perpetuate violence, and oppress women in faith communities. Research indicates ways in which ill-informed, but well-intentioned pastors and religious leaders use spirituality and religion to perpetuate violence through the misinterpretations of biblical scripture and religious tenants to justify intimate partner violence (Bent-Goodley & Fowler, 2006).

There is a great need to promote awareness among religious leaders and congregants experiencing IPV about the specific ways in which spirituality and religion can be manipulated to become a tool of abuse and oppression for women (Bent-Goodley & Fowler, 2006). This occurrence can be remedied by educating faith-based communities and their religious and spiritual leaders on problem of IPV, the ways in which spiritual and religious abuse affects IPV survivors, women and children, and the impact of family violence within the faith community. This may serve to encourage religious and spiritual leaders and congregants to gain a better understanding of IPV, elicit a response to the problem that overtly condemns family violence, and holds perpetrators accountable.

Additionally, educating religious and spiritual leaders on faith-based IPV education, and culturally competent approaches to identifying, assessing, and responding to IPV, will serve to promote IPV awareness, and provide empowerment, education and resources to IPV survivors.

Despite the connection of religious and spiritual involvement in coping, and mental health outcomes, few culturally competent utilizing these components, have been developed to address IPV survivors within the Africa American community.

To provide religions leaders and mental health professionals with culturally appropriate tools to rigorously address this serious issue, Fearless and Free to BE offers comprehensive training curricula to educate religious leaders about IPV and issues of spiritual and religious abuse. The manual assists group leaders in facilitating IPV psycho-education/ process groups substantiated by biblical scripture and Christian doctrine, in order to promote awareness, guidance and holistic healing to African American women experiencing IPV. In addition to psycho-educational material, this manual equips group leaders with discussion topics, process questions, and activities geared toward increasing awareness and furthering discussion.

This culturally relevant approach combines the proven efficacy of communal support, psycho-education and a faith based approach to facilitate empowerment, emotional and psychological healing, spiritual development, and resilience for survivors in minority communities. This faith-based approach can be utilized in a variety of religious institutions and clinical settings, and would be beneficial to the field of mental health.

Introduction

Fearless and Free to BE is a faith-based (Christian) group curriculum and instructors manual designed to equip religious leaders and mental health professionals with sophisticated tools to recognize and effectively respond to intimate partner violence within minority communities of faith. Fearless and Free to BE is intended to allow faith-based leaders and mental health clinicians to deliver Christian based group IPV education to African American female adult survivors of IPV within their faith communities. Qualified religious leaders utilizing the manual within their churches, and mental health professional collaborating with churches in the African American community should make an informed decision to conduct the group in a safe space that would cater to confidentiality within the church setting. The sensitive nature of IPV calls for an environment that is tailored to privacy and safety within the church. Furthermore, the manual can be used within religious institutions, and various clinical settings.

The manual describes a 12-week 90 minute Christian based IPV group curriculum. Each 90 minute group session is described in detail with specific instructions for group facilitators to promote IPV awareness, and impart to survivors skills to recognize patterns of abuse in relationships, education on scriptural and religious abuse, safety planning, empowerment and spiritual healing. Weekly topics include an introduction to IPV, warning signs, components and behavioral patterns of abuse, provision of resources, safety planning strategies, support system development, and fostering healthy relationships with the self and others. Topics of exploration will also focus on examining the perspective of the perpetrators of violence, characteristics of male abusers, and the impacts of abuse on children and parenting in family violence. The last group session includes a sharing of experiences, reflections on knowledge gained throughout the group series, and providing feedback to religious group facilitators. Each of the 12 90-minute weekly group sessions is structured to include:

1. Instructions to Group Leaders
2. Check-In Procedures
3. Presentation of material and related Activity
4. Positive affirmation readings and reflection
5. Scriptural and faith-based affirmation readings and reflection
6. An opportunity to share personal experiences with others in group

OVERVIEW OF FEARLESS AND FREE TO BE GROUP CURRICULUM

Session 1: Weeks 1-2

Instructions to Group Facilitators

In the first session, the purpose, overview, structure of the group, group rules, and course outline are presented. Most of the session is spent presenting information, verifying that the group members understand the information, and handing out copies of group syllabi and group rules. Then the facilitator takes the group members through an introductory exercise and a presentation of the domestic violence True/ False Quiz, definition of domestic violence, types of abuse, affect of spiritual and religious abuse within faith communities, and Myths and Facts of abuse.

Outline of Weeks 1&2:
• **Instructions to Group Facilitators**
• **Opening Prayer**
• **Scriptural Affirmation Quotes**
• **Suggested Commentary**
• **Purpose and Overview**
• **Group Rules**
• **True or False Quiz**
• **Myths and Facts of IPV**
• **Defining DV/ Stats**
• **Member Introductions**
• **Scriptural Affirmations**
• **Positive Affirmations**

Suggested Commentary

(Present the following script, or put this in your own words.)

Purpose and Overview

The purpose of Fearless and Free to BE is to:

1. Learn skills to recognize patterns of abuse in relationships
2. Learn safety planning skills
3. Gain a comprehensive understanding of relationship abuse dynamics and the different types of abuse, including spiritual and religious abuse
4. Build self-esteem and self-worth through faith development and spiritual growth
5. Develop skills to access internal resources, develop a healthy social support network, and utilize external resources

Group Rules

1. Group Safety: No violence, threats, derogatory comments, or foul language toward the facilitator and group members are allowed. It is imperative that members perceive the group as a safe atmosphere to share their experiences and feelings without threats, physical harm, or emotional damage.

2. Confidentiality: Group members should not discuss outside the group what group members say during the group sessions. Particularly, names of group members, and experiences discussed are not to be repeated outside of the group. While members are free to discuss their own personal inner experience, it is crucial that members refrain from sharing the experience and stories of other members and do not use names of members outside of the group. There is no exception to this component of the rule, as confidentiality is implemented to prevent imminent danger to any member of the group. There are, however limits to confidentiality. Health laws in the State of California govern how and when professionals must report certain actions to the proper authorities. Such actions include any disclosure indicating the knowledge of child abuse or the intent of homicide or suicide. Reporting abuse of these persons supersedes confidentiality laws involving group members and group facilitators. Similarly, if group member makes threats to physically harm or kill another person, the group leader is required, under the Tarasoff Ruling, to warn the intended victims and notify the police.

3. Check-Ins: These are to be performed by each group member in the beginning of every meeting. Each group member is given a Feelings Form [see IDV 0B: Check-In: "How Do You Feel Today," in Appendix B] that lists several feeling words. Members are to circle the feeling word that they are experiencing in the present moment and articulate what they are feeling and a brief explanation for their feelings. Members use the same sheet each group meeting and should use a different colored pen or highlighter to mark the feelings each session. Each member should also provide each date in the same color corresponding with the date when particular feelings words were marked. Group members must also put their names on the forms. The basis is to allow members to visibly track the differences in their Here and Now feelings and their awareness of their inner experience as the meetings progress. After Check-Ins are completed in the beginning of session, group members will always need to collect the Feelings Forms from the group members. The group facilitator will need to file group members Check-Ins in a secure location onsite, in a locked file cabinet for confidentiality reasons, and must always remember to bring in each of the

Feelings forms and give them back to the appropriate group member each session only for the Check-In portion of the meeting. Again, after the Check-In session is over, group facilitators must collect and securely store the Feelings Forms.

4. Homework Assignments: Brief homework assignments will be given each week. The homework will never include tangible or physical paperwork, in order to ensure the safety of each member who may be put in imminent danger by bringing evidence of their participating in a domestic violence group. However, homework will consist of mental reflections of class discussions and activities, reflections of daily affirmations, safety planning, social support development, and utilization of available resources.

5. Absences and Cancellations: Members should call or otherwise notify the group facilitator in advance when they cannot attend a session. Because of the amount of material presented in each session, members must not miss more than three sessions. If a group member misses more than three sessions, she would not be able to adequately learn, practice and apply the concepts and skills taught in the group. She can continue to attend the group sessions but will need to make up the specific missed sessions during the next group series.

6. Timeout: The group facilitator reserves the right to call for a timeout or a group prayer. If a group member's affect begins to escalate in extreme anger, depression, hostility, and/or any otherwise disruptive emotional display that impedes the progression of the group, the group facilitator will ask that member to take a timeout from the topic and the discussion. This means that the member, along with the rest of the members of the group, will immediately stop talking about the issue that is causing the member's emotional dysregulation. If the member has escalated to the point that she cannot tolerate sitting in the group, the leader may ask the person to leave the group for 5 to 10 minutes or until she can cool down. The group member is then welcomed back to the group, provided she can tolerate continued discussion in the group. Failure to comply with the timeout rule may lead to termination from the group.

Introduction to Domestic Violence: Historical Background

Historically, in the Roman times as well as in the fourteenth through the seventeenth centuries in European countries and North America, a wife was viewed as the property of her husband. Husbands were permitted to punish and discipline their wives through corporal punishment. Laws have sanctioned spousal abuse and, more specifically, wife abuse. The expression "Rule of Thumb" came from the old British legal system which stipulated that the wife was the property of her husband and that punishment of her was his responsibility and right. Thus a husband could take whatever means he saw fit, as long as the instrument of punishment was no thicker than his thumb.

History has revealed that over one million women were executed as witches and were victims of atrocities for having miscarriages, for adultery, and for speaking out against men and doctrines of the church.

Partially adapted from Encyclopedia of Domestic Violence, N.A. Jackson. New York: Routledge: Taylor & Francis Group.

Defining Domestic Violence: Some Operational Definitions

Domestic abuse, also known as intimate partner abuse or as spousal abuse, occurs when one person in an intimate relationship or marriage tries to dominate or control the other person though a pattern of threatening and abusive behaviors. Whenever one person uses force to control or hurt another person's body, mind, or spirit—this is abuse. Domestic abuse that includes physical violence is called *domestic violence* or *intimate partner violence*.

Domestic violence and abuse are used for the purpose of gaining and maintaining total and complete control over you. A perpetrator uses fear, guilt, shame, and intimidation and manipulation to maintain control over you. Your abuser may also threaten you, hurt you, or hurt those close to you, including your children.

Domestic violence and abuse does not discriminate. It occurs with heterosexual couples and in same-sex partnerships. It occurs within all age ranges, ethnic backgrounds, and economic levels. Abusive behavior is never acceptable, whether it is coming from a man, a woman, a teenager, or an older adult. You deserve to feel valued, respected, and safe.

Domestic violence does not go away on its own. It tends to get worse and become more frequent and more severe with time. The effect on children from witnessing the violence can be devastating, and without intervention can cause severe problems.

Adapted from Smith, M and Segal, J. (February 2014). Help Group Organization. In Domestic Violence and Abuse: Signs of Abuse and Abusive Relationships. http://www.helpgroup.org

Defining Spiritual & Religious Abuse and the Unique Role for Leaders to Respond to Domestic Violence

Spiritual and religious abuse is something that does occur in religious institutions. While there are many religious leaders who continue to be a source of spiritual counsel to their congregant members, there are ways in which well-meaning leaders unintentionally facilitate spiritual and religions abuse. In many cases, patriarchal ideologies that sanction male dominance and female submissiveness in faith communities may legitimate or fail to adequately condemn domestic violence, despite the severity and prevalence of the issue (Nason-Clark, 2000). Strong beliefs about the sanctity of marriage and the vows taken before God may be upheld in the face of a woman's personal safety, due to the lack of awareness and understanding about the seriousness and prevalence of domestic violence (DV). The church, with historical curative presence in the Black community, has the power to address the issue of violence and intervene. Studies reveal reduced likelihood of substance abuse and psychological problems among DV survivors as a result of indirect positive effects of the Black church (i.e., increased social support through rituals, sermons, and informal social interactions). Certainly, the church can embody a protective factor against the perpetration of DV (Ellison & Anderson, 2001).

There is a need for church leaders and congregants to educate themselves about DV and how it affects their congregants. Religious leaders must also enhance their understanding of how spiritual and religious abuse affects survivors of DV, both women and children, and the impact of family violence on the faith environment, with congregants who may perceive the pandemic of DV as either acceptable or largely ignored and under-acknowledged within the faith community. With further education and awareness of the specific ways in which the church "can have a positive impact on families who are being destroyed by the vestiges of violence and oppression" (Bent- Goodley & Fowler, 2006, p. 292), faith-based leaders can be fully equipped to fuel the movement of eradicating domestic violence in the faith community.

By facilitating DV awareness and identifying specific ways that spirituality and religion can be manipulated as instruments of oppression, women can be empowered and affirmed that it is not their spiritual integrity that is in question but the very ways in which spirituality can be inadvertently used as a tool of oppression (Bent-Goodley & Fowler, 2006). Religious leaders can have the unique role of responding to domestic violence and exposing the violence for what it is by facilitating discourse to challenge gender oppression associated with distorted misinterpretations of scripture, and fervently addressing an issue within the faith community.

> As part of our collective self-recovery African Americans must once again courageously interrogate religious and spiritual practice that stands in the way of healthy self-esteem while simultaneously seeking out those forms of religious worship and spiritual practice that affirm the integrity of our being. (Hooks, 2003, p. 117)

Handouts

- IDV 0: Course Outline
- IDV 0A: Group Rules
- IDV 0B: Check-Ins
- IDV 0C: Positive and Spiritual Affirmations
- IDV 1A: True or False Quiz
- IDV 1B: Defining DV
- IDV 1C: Myths and Facts
- IDV 2A: Types of Abuse
- IDV 2B: DV and the Church
- IDV 2C: Religious and Spiritual Abuse

Topics for Group Discussion

1. Provide an overview of IDV 0-Course Outline, discussing the purpose and structure of the group.
2. Review IDV 0A: Group Rules, being sure to confirm that each member in the group acknowledges and agrees to the group rules.
3. Review IDV 0B: Check-Ins, ensure that each member is aware Check-Ins are to be done in the beginning of each group meeting.
4. Have the group member complete IDV 1A: True or False quiz to the best of their abilities prior to any new information. After group members complete the quiz, go over each answer with the group.
5. Go over handout IDV 1B: Defining DV and allow members to articulate their idea of what domestic violence is. Ask the group members to reflect on the historical context of DV and what it means to them.
6. Go over handout IDV 1C: Myths & Facts and ask the group members to try to determine and articulate the myths from the facts before proving group members with the answers

7. Go over handout IDV 2A: Types OF Abuse and allow members to provide examples of different types of abuse
8. Go over handout IDV 2B: DV & the Church and allow members to articulate their thoughts and beliefs and experiences as it pertains to the church and domestic violence in their specific experiences
9. Go over handout 1DV 2C: Religious and Spiritual Abuse

Closing

- Opportunity to share personal experience with others in the group
- Selected readings from scriptural and faith-based daily affirmations
- Homework assignment
- Closing prayer

SHATTERING THE CYCLE:

DECONSTRUCTING THE DYNAMICS OF ABUSE

Session 2 : Weeks 3-4

Instructions to Group Facilitators

This session teaches group members about the dynamics of domestic violence, the power and control wheel, and the cycle of violence. It assists group members in identifying and understanding patterns of abuse. Begin this session with an opening prayer. Immediately after, have each group member provide a brief group check-in (a report of predominant current emotion). Following check-in, facilitate affirmation readings and then proceed to recap previous week's topic and follow up on any homework assignment from the last week.

Suggested Commentary

(Present the following script, or put this in your own words.)

Recap Previous Week:

Purpose of Fearless and Free to BE, group rules, previous week topic-historical context of DV, operational definitions, myths and facts, types of abuse, spiritual and religious abuse, homework assignment follow-up.

Explaining the Check-In Procedure

Go over instructions for individual check-ins, affirmation readings, and necessity for opening and closing prayers

Outline of Weeks 3&4
• **Instructions to Group Facilitators**
• **Opening Prayer**
• **Group Member Check-ins**
• **Scriptural Affirmation Quotes**
• **Suggested Commentary**
• **Review of Previous Week's Material**
• **Power & Control Wheel**
• **Equality Wheel**
• **Healthy Relationships**
• **Positive Affirmations**
• **Closing Prayer**

Handouts

- BTC 1A: Dynamics of Power & Control
- BTC 1B: Power & Control Wheel
- BTC 1C: Power & Control Wheel Wkst 1
- BTC 2A: Cycle of Violence
- BTC 2B: Cycle of Violence Wkst 1
- BTC 3A: Equality Wheel
- BTC 3B: Healthy Relationship Article 1

Topics for Group Discussion

1. Facilitate exploration and inquiry of group's perception of the underlying components of DV.
2. Go over handout BTC 1A: Dynamics of Power & Control. Allow members to share their examples or thoughts on components of the dynamics of Power & Control
3. Go over handout BTC 1C: Power & Control Wheel. Allow members to share their understanding of each component of the wheel and their thoughts, reflections and examples.
4. Go over instructions for BTC 1C: Worksheet Vignette. Have members take turns reading a vignette and allow members first to identify and write down the type of power and control from the wheel and then substantiate it with examples from the vignette.
5. Go over BTC 2A: Cycle of Violence. Have members take turns reading the quotes and scenarios in BTC 2B: Cycle of Violence Wkst, and allow members to discuss their answers.
6. Allow members to share and explore their perceptions, feelings, examples, thoughts about what makes a healthy relationship.
7. Go over handout BTC 3A: Equality Wheel. Proceed with BTC 3B: Worksheet Article similarly to activity in step #4. Allow members to reading article "Equally Yoked" and identify components of the Equality Wheel found in the article and substantiate with examples from the article.

Closing

- Opportunity to share personal experience with others in the group
- Selected readings from scriptural and faith-based daily affirmations
- Selected readings from positive affirmations
- Homework assignment
- Closing prayer

UNDERSTANDING, ELEVATING AND EQUIPPING THE SURVIVOR:

ON THE PATH TO FEARLESS AND FREE

Session 3: Weeks 5-6

Instructions to Group Facilitators

This session offers teachings about the reasons domestic violence survivors often stay in abusive relationships, safety planning, provision of available resources and how to access resources, and social support development. It assists group members in gaining insight into their struggles in leaving abusive relationships, refuting distorted and false beliefs about self-image, and refuting cognitive distortions as it relates to domestic abuse. Begin this session with an opening prayer. Immediately after, have each group member provide a brief group check-in (a report of predominant current emotion). Following check-in, facilitate affirmation readings, and then proceed to recap previous week's topic and a follow up on any homework assignment from the last week.

Outline of Weeks 5&6
• **Instructions to Group Facilitators**
• **Opening Prayer**
• **Group Member Check-ins**
• **Scriptural Affirmation Quotes**
• **Suggested Commentary**
• **Review of Previous Week's Material**
• **Why We Stay**
• **Safety Planning**
• **Positive Affirmations**
• **Closing Prayer**

Suggested Commentary

(Present the following script, or put this in your own words.)

Recap Previous Week:

1. Dynamics of Power & Control in abusive relationships, Power & Control Wheel, Equality Wheel, Healthy Relationships, homework assignment follow-up.
2. Explain the check-in procedure.
3. Review instructions for individual check-ins, affirmation readings, and necessity for opening and closing prayers.

Handouts

- UTV 1: Self Reflection/Why I Stayed
- UTV 2A: Reasons Why She Stays
- UTV 2B: Why Doesn't She Leave Role-Play Script
- UTV 3A: Safety Planning Check List
- UTV 3B: Thinking About Leaving

Topics for Group Discussion

1. Allow members to complete handout UTV 1: Self Reflection/Why I Stayed and voluntarily share their reflections. Facilitate exploration of group member perceptions of why women often stay in abusive relationships.

2. Go over handout UTV 2A: Reasons Why She Stays and facilitate open discussion on thoughts, reflections, or examples of each of the reasons.

3. Facilitate group activity UTV 2B-Role Play Script. Allow members to pick a role to play from the script and act out the role-play. Facilitate open discussion of the role-play, allowing members to identify the reasons the DV victim in the script stayed in her abusive relationship. Allow members to write down the answers on their handout.

4. Go over handout UTV 3A: Safety Planning Check List and facilitate open discussion regarding what should be included in a safety plan.

5. Go over handout UTV 3B: Thinking About Leaving and facilitate dialogue about common questions and concerns about leaving abusive relationships, accessing available resources.

Closing

- Opportunity to share personal experience with others in the group
- Selected readings from scriptural and faith-based daily affirmations
- Homework assignment
- Closing prayer

UNDERSTANDING, DISMANTLING, AND DEMPOWERING THE ABUSER

Session 4: Weeks 7-8

Instructions to Group Facilitators

This session teaches group members about the characteristics and common myths about DV perpetrators and allows group members to apply their new knowledge to realistic vignettes. Begin this session with an opening prayer. Next, have each group member provide a brief group check-in (a report of predominant current emotion). Following check-in, facilitate affirmation readings and then proceed to recap previous week's topic and follow up on any homework assignment from the last week.

Suggested Commentary

(Present the following script, or put this in your own words.)

Recap Previous Week:

1. Reasons why many women choose to stay in abusive relationships, safety planning, homework assignment follow-up.
2. Explaining the check-in procedure
3. Go over instructions for individual check-ins, affirmation readings, and necessity for opening and closing prayers

Handouts

- EA 1: Myths About Abusers
- EA 2: Characteristics of Abusive Men
- EA 2A: Characteristics of Abusive Men
- EA 3: Into the Mind of a DV Perpetrator True of False Quiz

Outline of Weeks 7&8

- **Instructions to Group Facilitators**
- **Opening Prayer**
- **Group Member Check-ins**
- **Scriptural Affirmation Quotes**
- **Suggested Commentary**
- **Review of Previous Week's Material**
- **Identifying Abusers**
- **Countering Myths**
- **Vignette on Abusers**
- **DV Abuser Quiz**
- **Positive Affirmations**
- **Closing Prayer**

Topics for Group Discussion

1. Provide group members with EA 1: Myths. Facilitate open discussion about the myths and group members' thoughts, reflections, about the myths.
2. Go over handout EA 2 and facilitate open discussion about the characteristics of abusers. Go over handout BTC 1C: Power & Control Wheel. Allow members to share their understanding of each component of the wheel, their thoughts, reflections and examples.
3. Go over instructions for EA 2A Worksheet vignette and allow members to take turns reading each vignette and then allow members to identify examples of characteristics of abusive men in the vignettes.
4. Go over instructions for EA 1: Quiz. Allow each member to complete the quiz on their own. After members have completed the quiz, facilitate a collective review of the answers.

Closing

- Opportunity to share personal experience with others in the group
- Selected readings from scriptural and faith-based daily affirmations
- Homework Assignment
- Closing Prayer

FRAGMENTATION OF THE FAMILY IN VIOLENCE:

IMPACT OF ABUSE IN THE HOME

Session 5: Weeks 9-10

Instructions to Group Facilitators

This session teaches group members the devastating effects of abuse in the home as it relates to children and parenting. It also educates members about effective parenting after experiencing DV. It also facilitates open discussion and exploration of better parenting strategies to mitigate the effects of abuse and help bring about healing in children. Begin this session with an opening prayer. Next, have each group member provide a brief group check-in (a report of predominant current emotion). Following check-in, facilitate affirmation readings, and then proceed to recap previous week's topic and follow up on any homework assignment from the last week.

Outline of Weeks 9&10
• **Instructions to Group Facilitators**
• **Opening Prayer**
• **Group Member Check-ins**
• **Scriptural Affirmation Quotes**
• **Suggested Commentary**
• **Review of Previous Week's Material**
• **Abuse & Family Dynamics**
• **Abuser Checklist**
• **Abusive & Parenting**
• **Red Flags**
• **Self-defeating Thoughts**
• **Positive Affirmations**
• **Closing Prayer**

Suggested Commentary

(Present the following script, or put this in your own words.)

Recap Previous Week:

Characteristics of abusive men, countering myths, homework assignment follow-up

Explaining the Check-in Procedure

Go over instructions for individual check-ins, affirmation readings, and necessity for opening and closing prayers

Handouts

- IOA 1: Abusive Men Affect Family Dynamics
- IOA 2: Abuser Checklist
- IOA 3: How Abusive Men Parent
- IOA 4: Red Flags
- IOA 5: Self-Defeating Thoughts

Topics for Group Discussion

1. Go over handout IOA: Abusive Men Affect Family Dynamics and allow members to complete the handout and voluntarily share their reflections. Facilitate exploration of group member perceptions of how abuse affects family dynamics.
2. Go over handout IOA 2: Abuser Checklist and facilitate open discussion on thoughts, reflections, or examples of items on the checklist.
3. Go over handout IOA 3: How Abusive Men Parent. Facilitate discussion on parenting tendencies evident in abusive men.
4. Go over handout IOA 4: Red Flags and facilitate open discussion regarding various red flags.
5. Go over handout IOA 5: Self-Defeating Thoughts and facilitate dialogue about self-defeating thoughts, with emphasis on the destructive nature of these thoughts and identification of counter thoughts/ realistic self- appraisals.

Closing

- Opportunity to share personal experience with others in the group
- Selected readings from scriptural and faith-based daily affirmations
- Selected readings from positive affirmations
- Homework assignment
- Closing prayer

LIVING FEARLESS AND FREE:
CELEBRATING YOUR JOURNEY TO FREEDOM

Session 6: Weeks 11-12

Instructions to Group Facilitators

This is the last session meeting and will reinforce what group members have learned throughout the group series through final exam and a review of key concepts. This session will also allow for development of social support networks through social and communal activities during the group. Begin this session with an opening prayer. Next, have each group member provide a brief check-in (a report of predominant current emotion). Following check-in, facilitate affirmation readings, then proceed to recap previous week's topic and follow up any homework assignment from the last week. Each group member can now review and keep her check-in Feelings Form to track progression of feelings.

Suggested Commentary

(Present the following script, or put this in your own words.)

Recap Previous Week:

> The impact of abuse on family dynamics, violence in the home, impact of abuse on children, effective parenting to mitigate effects of abuse, red flags, self-defeating thoughts homework assignment follow-up.

Explaining the Check-in Procedure

> Go over instructions for individual check-ins, affirmation readings, and necessity for opening and closing prayers.

Outline of Weeks 11&12
- Instructions to Group Facilitators
- Opening Prayer
- Group Member Check-ins
- Scriptural Affirmation Quotes
- Suggested Commentary
- Review of Previous week's Material
- Final Exam
- Review of Exam Answers
- Reflection of group
- Group Activity
- Self-defeating Thoughts
- Positive Affirmations
- Closing Prayer

Handouts

- C 1: Final Exam
- C 2: Get To Know You

Topics for Group Discussion

1. This will be a time to wrap up, share experiences, provide feedback to facilitators, and celebrate with those who have completed the course.
2. Allow members to complete handout C 1: Final Exam individually during group. When all the group members have completed the exam, allow members to collectively go over the answers.
3. Facilitate open discussion on thoughts, reflections, or examples of the exam; of the group in general; and of each member's feeling of personal growth, sense of esteem and worth and their personal commitment to themselves, including but not limited to, leaving or avoiding abusive relationships, developing their spirituality, building their social support network, accessing available resources, maintaining daily practice of utilizing positive affirmations and spiritual affirmations, increasing church attendance, etc.
4. Facilitate group activity C 2: Get to Know You. Allow members to pick a partner to interview, answer the interview questions, and present their partner to the group.

Closing

- Opportunity to share personal experience with others in the group
- Selected readings from scriptural and faith based daily affirmations
- Homework assignment
- Closing prayer

APPENDIX B

Handouts For Fearless and Free to Be
Group Sessions

The handouts on the following pages are to be used by group members within the group and with the facilitator's guidance. The handouts will help members of the group make the most of the weekly group meetings.

IDV O: COURSE OUTLINE

Fearless and Free to BE

Faith-Based Group Curriculum on Intimate Partner Violence:

Group Outline

Date:

Time:

Facilitators:

_____

_____

Class Description:

Fearless and Free to BE is a group curriculum implemented to equip intimate partner violence survivors with skills to recognize patterns of abuse in relationships, understand different aspects of relationship abuse and to educate survivors about spiritual and religious abuse as it pertains to domestic violence. The class consists of 12 weekly group sessions. Each class session will include:

- Opening prayer
- A recap of the previous week's topic and reading of our biblically based affirmations
- Presentation of information or material about a new topic
- Interactive activity and discussion related to the day's topic
- An opportunity to share personal experiences with others in group
- An inspirational quote to take with you during the week
- Closing prayer

Because each class builds upon the last, please do your best to attend class as regularly as possible.

Goals:

We hope that by the end of the quarter, each member of the class will leave with:

1. A greater understanding of what domestic violence is and what the various types of abuse look like.
2. An ability to preserve their safety and well-being by recognizing and identifying precursors of an abusive relationship before entering the cycle of abuse.
3. Cultivate a sense of empowerment in taking control of their lives.

Schedule:

The facilitators will keep to the schedule as closely as possible, but if there are unforeseen circumstances, changes may be made.

Section 1: Overview of Fearless and Free to BE curriculum

Talking About Abuse

- What is domestic violence/ intimate partner violence?
- Myths and Facts: What's really true?

The Many Faces of Abuse

- Discovering the different types of abuse
- Discovering Religious and Spiritual abuse

Section 2: Shattering the Cycle

Understanding the Role of Control

- Power and control wheel Vs Equality Wheel

When Abuse Becomes a Pattern

- Cycle of violence

Section 3: Understanding and Elevating the Survivor

Leaving Is Difficult

- Uncovering the reasons why women may stay in violent relationships

Section 4: Equipping the Survivor

- Continued discussion on why women stay in violent relationships
- Safety planning and how to get out

Section 5: Understanding, Dismantling & Disempowering the Abuser

Profile of an Abuser

- Characteristics of male abusers
- Part 2- Continued discussion on characteristics of male abusers

Section 6: Fragmentation of the Family in Violence

Abuse Affects Everyone

- Violence in the home
- Part 2- Continued discussion on violence in the home

Moving Forward

- Parenting after experiencing abuse

Celebrating Your Journey to Live Fearless and Free to BE!

- Reinforce skills and knowledge through final exam
- Develop positive social support system
- This will be a time to wrap up, share experiences, provide feedback to facilitators, and celebrate with those who have completed the course.

IDV 0A: GROUP RULES

Group Rules

- Maintain **co**nfidentiality outside of the group: Do not discuss what is said during group sessions or disclose names of group members outside of the group. What happens in group STAYS in group!

- Group Safety: No violence, threats, derogatory comments or foul language toward the facilitator and group members is allowed.

- Be on time. However, for absences and cancellations, members should call or otherwise notify group facilitator 24 hours in advance if she cannot attend session. If a group member misses more than 3 sessions she will need to make up the specific missed sessions.

- Stay for the remainder of group, don't leave early!

- No cell phones.

- Participate, don't dominate!

- Respect others in group by not interrupting or having side conversations.

- Be culturally sensitive by respecting differences.

IDV 0B: CHECK-IN

Name _____ Date _____

How Do You Feel Today?

Pleasant Feelings

Open, confident, accepting, receptive, satisfied, free, amazed, understood, happy, joyous, proud, fortunate, delighted, overjoyed, grateful, worthy, important, lively, valued, glad, cheerful, elated, appreciative, alive, appreciated, energetic, positive, liberated, courageous, playful, optimistic, impulsive, calm, peaceful, patient, at ease, relieved, respected, comfortable, encouraged, surprised, secure, content, relaxed, blessed, reassured, loving, empathetic, loved, considerate, caring, affectionate, devoted, loyal, passionate, trusting, self-reliant, compassionate, comforted, concerned, fascinated, absorbed, inquisitive, eager, curious, lovable, fearless, fixated, inspired, determined, excited, relentless, enthusiastic, bold, brave, daring, hopeful, pleased, vulnerable, re-energized, preoccupied, nonchalant, generous_____

Difficult/ Unpleasant Feelings

Withdrawn, misunderstood, alone, sensitive, empty, numb, anxious, weak, overwhelmed, challenged, isolated, defeated, cautious, disorganized, broken, frustrated, tense, uneasy, defensive, enraged, annoyed, angry, worried, hateful, uncomfortable, resentful, unloved, envious, sad, disappointed, ashamed, rejected, nervous, helpless, diminished, guilty, dissatisfied, revengeful, distraught, doubtful, confused, humiliated, pressured, hesitant, insecure, awkward, judgmental, shallow, regretful, distrustful, lost, unsure, suspicious, incapable, fragile, trapped, sorrowful, exhausted, inadequate, useless, inferior, exposed, distressed, rebellious, worked up, hopeless, callous, apathetic, fearful, timid, restless, threatened, tormented, deprived, hurt, heartbroken, lonely, out-of-control, self-loathing, embarrassed_____

IDV 1A: QUIZ 1

Delving into Domestic Violence (DV)

True or False Quiz

DV only involves physical abuse.	True	False
DV does not affect women of all racial and socioeconomic backgrounds.	True	False
It has been reported that DV affects more than 5 million American women annually.	True	False
85% to 95% of reported DV survivors are women.	True	False
Research identifies DV as the number one health issue among African American women.	True	False
While physical and sexual violence are forms of domestic abuse, emotional and economic abuse are not considered components of DV.	True	False
DV victimization can have wide ranging long term effects, and those who with abusive partners are at an increased risk for developing mental health problems, such as depression, anxiety and PTSD.	True	False
Using isolation is not included on the Power and Control Wheel as a component of DV	True	False
DV affects all individuals and communities, adults and teenagers, regardless of race, culture, ethnicity, socioeconomic status, or religion	True	False

IDV 1B: DEFINING DV

DOMESTIC VIOLENCE HISTORY

Domestic violence has not always been against the law. In fact, it is a relatively recent law that states battery against one's spouse is illegal. Even with this law in place, it is still sometimes difficult to press charges and receive justice in even severe cases of spousal abuse. In 1986, police officers were given the right to press charges if spousal abuse was observed, even if the spouse did not press charges. The reason for this is partly due to the acknowledgement of a type of PTSD called Battered Women Syndrome. In many cases, victims of domestic violence experience this syndrome, which often inhibits the battered partner to press charges.

Domestic violence does not exclusively occur in male to female battering situations. Cases where battering against a male partner by a woman do exist. However, research indicates that about 97% of partner abuse cases are male to female battering. Case in point, the focus of the curriculum targets male to female domestic violence.

DV DEFINITION:

Domestic violence is a pattern of abusive and threatening behaviors including physical violence, emotional abuse, economic abuse, sexual violence, intimidation, isolation, and coercion directed at achieving and maintaining power and control over an intimate partner.

Adapted from American Bar Association, "Know your Rights: Domestic Violence." (2001)

DV STATISTICS:

- Boys who grow up in violent homes are more likely to grow up to be abusive partners as adults.
- 4,000 women die each year as a result of beatings.
- In 60% of violent homes where the female partner is beaten, so are the children.
- Around the world, at least one in every three women has been beaten, coerced into sex or otherwise abused during her lifetime. Most often, the abuser is a member of her own family.

- Domestic violence is the leading cause of injury to women—more than car accidents, muggings, and rapes combined.
- Studies suggest that up to 10 million children witness some form of DV annually.
- Every day in the U.S., more than three women are murdered by their husbands or boyfriends.
- Domestic violence victims lose nearly 8 million days of paid work per year in the US alone—the equivalent of 32,000 full-time jobs.
- Based on reports from 10 countries, between 55 percent and 95 percent of women who had been physically abused by their partners had never contacted nongovernmental organizations, shelters, or the police for help.
- The costs of intimate partner violence in the US alone exceed $5.8 billion per year: $4.1 billion are for direct medical and health care services, while productivity losses account for nearly $1.8 billion.
- Men who as children witnessed their parents' domestic violence were twice as likely to abuse their own wives as sons of nonviolent parents were.
- Battered women have twice as many miscarriages as non-battered women.

Source:
"Domestic Violence Statistics: Let's Put a Stop to Domestic Violence and Abuse." (2014) Domestic Violence Statistics Organization. http://domesticviolencestastics.org/domestic-violence-statistics/.

IDV 1C: MYTHS & FACTS

MYTHS & FACTS ABOUT DOMESTIC VIOLENCE

MYTH	FACT
DV is very rare and only affects a small percentage of the population.	• 1 in 4 women will experience DV in her life time. • An estimated 1.3 million women are victims of physical assault by an intimate partner each year, according to national studies.
DV is not a serious problem in the U.S.	• Domestic violence is the leading cause of injury to women between the ages of 15 and 44. • Almost one-third of female homicide victims that are reported in police records are killed by intimate partners. • 1,500 women are murdered as a result of domestic violence each year in the U.S. • Intimate partner violence results in more than 18.5 million mental health care visits each year • Approximately 1.5 million women are raped and or physically assaulted by an intimate partner each year (Tjaden and Thoennes, 2000) • There are 16,800 homicides and $2.2 million medically treated injuries due to intimate partner violence annually.
Only those who are poor, uneducated, or minorities experience domestic violence.	• Studies of domestic violence consistently have found that battering occurs among all types of families, regardless of economic status, race, ethnicity, or educational status. (Center for Disease Control and Prevention, 2013)

Alcohol consumption causes DV.	• While there is a high correlation between alcohol, substances and battering, alcohol does not cause or excuse the abuse. • Perpetrators use drinking as one of a number of excuses for their violence.
DV is usually a one-time, isolated event.	• Domestic violence is a pattern of abusive and violent behaviors that happens over and over again and escalates in severity and dangerousness. It is not just one physical attack. It includes the repeated use of various tactics as displayed on the Power & Control Wheel.
Men who commit domestic violence are often good fathers and have joint custody of their children when the couple separates.	• Studies have shown that men who commit domestic violence also abuse their children in 70% of the cases. • When children are not directly abused, they suffer as a result of witnessing one parent abuse another. According to a recent American Bar Association report, experts estimate that between 3.3 and 10 million children witness domestic violence annually. The report cites numerous links between serious emotional and psychological problems from exposure to domestic violence, such as depression, hopelessness, sleep disorders, violence towards other children, identifying with the aggressor, and losing respect for the victim (American Bar Association, 1995). • 30% to 60% of perpetrators of intimate partner violence also abuse children in the household • In a national survey of more than 6,000 American families, 50 % of men who abused their wives also abused their children.

Couples counseling is the best solution for DV.	• Couples counseling is not recommended for couples trying to end domestic violence in their relationship. • It is more beneficial and safe for abusers to attend a state certified family violence intervention program and for survivors to seek assistance from a domestic violence program or advocate.
Pregnant women are never victims of DV.	• National surveys indicate that 5.3% of pregnant women each year experience domestic violence. This means as many as 324,000 women experience intimate partner violence during pregnancy (Gazmararian, et al. 2000).
Religious people do not commit DV.	• Those who commit DV can be religious people, including clergy and other faith-based leaders. Many religious women who are victims of DV may feel obligated to stay in the abusive relationship and endure the violence, keeping the family together at all cost, because of deeply held religious beliefs.
DV against the mother never has an impact on the behaviors of the children who witnessed the abuse.	• Men who as children witness their fathers' abuse their mothers are twice as likely to abuse their wives as sons who have not witnessed abuse • A woman who witnesses her father abuse her mother has a much greater likelihood of becoming a battered woman herself (American Bar Association, 1995). • Children of DV are more likely to exhibit behavioral and physical health problems including, depression, anxiety, and violence towards peers. They are also more likely to attempt suicide, abuse alcohol and drugs, run away, commit sex crimes, and engage in prostitution (Futures Without Violence, 2014).

A person who abuses his wife or partner can only be considered abusive if he is also abusive in all his relationships with other people	• Most abusers do not use violence in other non-intimate relationships to resolve conflict. In fact, they typically present a different personality outside the home than they do inside. This often complicates a victim's ability to describe her experiences to other people outside the relationship when seeking help (Wilson, 1997).

Sources:

Saltzman, L. E., Johnson, C. H., Gilbert, B. C., Goodwin, M. M. (2003). Physical abuse around the time of pregnancy: An examination of prevalence and risk factors in 16 states. *Maternal and Child Health Journal*, *7*, 31-43.

Gazmararian, J., Petersen, R., Spitz, A., Goodwin, M., Saltzman, L., & Marks, J. (2000). Violence and reproductive health: Current knowledge and future research directions. *Maternal and Child Health Journal*, *4*(2), 79-84.

Wilson, K. J. (1997). When violence begins at home: A comprehensive guide to understanding and ending domestic abuse. Alameda, CA: Hunter House.

"Prevalence of Domestic Violence in the United States." (2014) Futures Without Violence Organization http://www.futureswithoutviolence.org

IDV 2A: TYPES OF ABUSE

TYPES OF ABUSE

PSYCHOLOGICAL & EMOTIONAL ABUSE

A perpetrator's use of emotional or psychological abuse can include persistent verbal abuse, harassment, excessive possessiveness, isolation from friends or family, invalidating of feelings, ignoring feelings, or other behaviors designed to rob the victim of self-esteem, lower her self-respect, and cause the victim to feel worthless.

Examples of abuse:

- Private and public humiliation, intimidation, degradation
- Deprivation of resources to meet basic needs
- Putting partner down, name-calling, labeling, ridiculing
- Demeaning jokes and insults
- Minimizing or denying abuse, blaming victim as the cause of the abuse
- Ignoring, ridiculing, constant criticizing, insulting, belittling and dismissing the partner's needs
- Eliminating partners support system, including friends, family, church, and others
- Threatening to take the children away or harm them or have DCFS take children from the mom
- Threats of harm or acts of violence/ injury to family and friends of partner, or partner's pets
- Intentionally destroying personal items belonging to partner
- Blaming partner for circumstances beyond her control, false accusations
- Demanding partner's constant attention
- Driving recklessly to frighten and intimidate the partner
- Resenting and/or preventing partner's attention to her children
- Leaving the partner in a dangerous place
- Refusing to help when the victim is sick or injured
- Using partner's children against partner
- Challenging partner's sense of reality
- Exhibiting extreme jealousy and possessiveness

PHYSICAL ABUSE

- Slapping, jerking, punching, pushing, showing, shaking, hitting, holding, restraining, choking, or strangling partner
- Pulling or twisting partner's hair, or dragging the partner by hair or body parts
- Leaving bruises on partner, lacerations, cutting, stabbing

- Throwing items at partner, threats and use of weapons such as guns or knives or household items
- Targeting hitting, punching, or kicking to specific body parts of partner's body
- Attempting to harm partner's unborn child through targeting abuse
- Deprivation of food, water, medical attention
- Restraining partner against will
- Physical abuse during pregnancy
- Imprisonment of partner in home, bedroom, basement
- Causing broken bones or internal injuries, or causing disabling, disfiguring, or permanent injury
- Committing murder

ECONOMIC ABUSE

The perpetrator tries to exert power and control over the victim through deprivation of all of her economic resources, causing the victim to be completely dependent on the perpetrator for her economic and financial well-being.

Examples of abuse:

- Making or controlling all partner's economic decisions
- Refusing to provide sufficient funds for economic needs such as gas, food, personal needs
- Deciding what partner's personal needs are and how much money she can spend for these needs
- Putting partner down, name-calling, labeling, ridiculing, degrading jokes and insults
- Minimizing or denying abuse, blaming victim as the cause of the abuse
- Eliminating partner's support system, including friends, family, church, and others
- Threatening to take the children away or harm them or have DCFS take children from the mom
- Threatening to harm family and friends of partner
- Intentionally destroying personal items belonging to partner
- Blaming partner for circumstances beyond her control
- Demanding partner's constant attention
- Resenting/preventing partner's attention to her children, using partner's children against partner
- Challenging partner's sense of reality

SEXUAL ABUSE

Sexual violence committed by the perpetrator often occurs in conjunction with physical attacks. The victim may be forced to engage in sexual intercourse, subjected to sexual taunts, or forced to engage in any form of sexual activity against her will.

Examples of abuse:

- Rape, use of threats to demand and receive sex, forced sexual acts
- Minimizing sexual abuse, labeling sexual abuse as consensual behavior
- Touching, grabbing, physically assaulting sexual body parts, molestation
- Demanding sex from partner even if medically inadvisable
- Physically hurting the victim during sex or assaulting her genitals, using objects or weapons to inflict pain
- Forcing partner to watch pornography, photographing partner while nude against partner's will
- Forcing partner into prostitution, forcing her to dress in a way that makes her uncomfortable
- Calling partner degrading sexual names
- Preventing partner's use of birth control
- Exposing partner to STDs through abuser's frequent affairs and refusal to use a condom or through coercing partner to have sex without protection against pregnancy or STDs.

Adapted from the following:

Women Against Abuse Organization (2010)
http://www.womenagainstabuse.org.

USDOJ, OJP, "Extent, Nature, and Consequences of Intimate Partner Violence: Findings From the National Violence Against Women Survey." 2000
Http://www.ovw.usdoj.gov/domestic violence.htm

What are some other examples of emotional, psychological, physical, economic and sexual types of abuse?

_____
_____
_____
_____
_____
_____
_____
_____

DOMESTIC VIOLENCE AND THE CHURCH

The Role of the Church

The church has played a prominent role in the African American cultural experience, fostering a sense of community, providing role models, and promoting healing through the channeling of collective spirituality and expression of faith. As anchors of the black experience, the Black church and spirituality have traditionally served as a medium to address "issues of oppression, quest for liberation, love, hope, and justice" (Anderson & Black, 1995). The church has historically embodied a source of coping, healing and empowerment, particularly in the African American community, and has served a range of functions such as supporting individual and collective self-help, racial socialization, and political mobilization throughout the U.S. (Lincoln & Mamiya, 1990). The research shows the positive influence of the church in the community as a source of guidance and support in areas such as relationships, family preservation, health initiatives, politics, education, and civil rights. It is clear that the church has been and continues to work as a positive force in the Black community, and can be a primary force to ending the epidemic of domestic violence in the Black community. The Black Church has the potential to provide African American women who experience intimate partner violence with the knowledge, guidance, and spiritual healing necessary to aid and empower survivors to develop a way out.

Traditional Approach to DV in the Church

- While the church has played a major role in promoting a means for those in the community deal with adversity, domestic violence has not always been directly addressed as a serious issue in the church (Potter, 2007).
- Though the Black church has the potential to address intimate partner violence and intervene in this significant issue, many religious leaders are not aware of the nature and severity of domestic violence and are therefore ill-equipped to identify and address the issue.
- Many in the church community are unaware that intimate partner violence is a growing epidemic in the African American community, and Black women experience higher rates of domestic violence and sustain serious and lethal

injuries than their Euro-American counterparts (Center for Disease Control and Prevention, 2000).

- Unfortunately, because of this lack of awareness, research shows that within the teachings of certain religious groups, abuse of women by their intimate partners is excused, and pastors are often complicit in the battering partners' behaviors.

- Many pastors and religious leaders often recommend a commonly referenced scripture pertaining to spousal relations that appears in the New Testament of the Bible, Ephesians 5:21-33, that helps perpetuate the control of women by their husbands.

- In a recent study, 40 self-identified African American intimate partner violence survivor participants sought counseling from religious leaders, suggesting the importance of clergy in supporting abused women. Eight of the 40 women reported substandard support from clergy members during their time of need and the pastoral advice to "remain in the relationship and 'work things out, . . . [to] pray about the relationship and make greater attempts to be a 'good wife'" (Potter, 2007, p. 272).

- Many women encounter rejection from faith-based leaders when they attempt to address domestic violence in their lives. Many report receiving messages to stay in the relationship, with justifications derived from misinterpretations of the Bible (Adams & Fortune, 1995).

Spiritual & Religious Abuse

Spiritual and religious abuse is something that does occur in religious institutions. While there are many faith-based, religious leaders who continue to be a source of spiritual counsel and ensure the well-being of their congregant members, there are ways in which well-meaning leaders unintentionally facilitate spiritual and religions abuse. In many cases, patriarchal ideologies that sanction male dominance and female submissiveness in faith communities may legitimize or fail to adequately condemn domestic violence, despite the severity and prevalence of the issue (Nason-Clark,1997 2000). Strong beliefs about the sanctity of marriage and the vows taken before God may be upheld in the face of a woman's personal safety. A lack of awareness and understanding about the epidemic of domestic violence in the Black community exists within the church. There is a need for church leaders and congregants to educate themselves about domestic violence and enhance their understanding of how congregants are affected by domestic violence as well as how spiritual and religious abuse affects DV survivors, both women and children, and the impact of family violence on the faith environment with congregants who may perceive the pandemic of domestic violence as either acceptable or largely ignored and under-acknowledged within the faith community. By facilitating DV awareness and identifying specific ways that spirituality and religion can be manipulated as instruments of oppression, women can be empowered and affirmed that it is not their spiritual integrity that is in question but instead the very ways in which spirituality can be inadvertently used as a tool of oppression (Bent-Goodley & Fowler, 2006).

Defining Spirituality and Religion

- Spirituality has been defined as "the sense of sacred and divine," emphasizing ones belief in God (Bent-Goodley & Fowler 2006, p. 291).
- Religion focuses on external expressions of faith, and external expressions of one's belief in God.
- Spirituality and religion are interconnected and often discussed interchangeably (Martin & Martin, 2002).
- Spirituality manifests as "a source of refuge and order" (Bent-Goodley & Fowler, 2006, p. 291).
- Spirituality also serves as a principal coping mechanism for achieving resilience in the face of adversity.

Spiritual & Religious Abuse

- Improper and negative use of scripture to manipulate and control women in domestic violence relationships, to justify abuse, and to perpetuate domestic violence
- The practice of "proof-texting" (selective use of a text, out of context, to support one's position) in justifying the abuser's actions, "thereby providing advice that supports the male perpetrator, whether the male abuser's behavior is publicly substantiated or rests on the accounts of the domestic violence survivor" (Potter, 2007, p. 2).
- Abuse with an impact that goes "beyond emotional and psychological damage to what supports the essence of the person" (Bent-Goodley & Fowler, 2006, p. 291), as reported by many DV survivors.
- Causing scripture to become a means of stimulating confusion and anger when it is misinterpreted, distorted, and used to manipulate and control a partner.
- Violating "spiritual integrity" by causing a partner to become unsure of the capability of God to evoke change in her life, while the partner is encouraged to forgive the abuser, pray for change and not abandon the relationship (Fortune, 1998; Nason-Clark, 2004).
- Using similar methods that an abuser uses to keep a woman in the abusive relationship in order to maintain relationship (i.e., evoking guilt by stressing the need to forgive, denying or minimizing the dangerousness of the abuse, and advising the woman to stay in the relationship regardless of the abuse) (Bent-Goodley & Fowler, 2006).
- Using religion and spirituality as contributors to women's vulnerability, which occurs when adherence to traditional roles of womanhood grounded in religious tenets (heterosexual relations, childbearing, childrearing and obeying the husband) are viewed as essential conditions of intimate unions, obligating women to subscribe to these conditions while being battered by an abusive partner (Potter, 2007).
- Causing a woman to question her own spiritual integrity and belief in God because of the actions of her abuser in light of pastoral guidance and advisement for her to stay in the abusive relationship and pray.

BTC 1A: DYNAMICS OF POWER & CONTROL

The Dynamics of Power & Control

Characteristics of a Batterer

Psychologists, social scientists and others have developed a number of theories to explain why some men use violence against women while others do not. These theories include:

- Growing up in dysfunctional families
- Inadequate communication and problem-solving skills
- Provocation by women
- Stress
- Chemical dependency
- Economic hardship and pressures

The National Coalition Against Domestic Violence (NCADV) asserts that although these issues may be associated with battering, they are not the cause of the behavior. As a result, removing these stressors from the batterer's life will not cease the violence. NCADV reports that "the batterer begins and continues his behavior because violence is an effective method for gaining and keeping control over another person and he usually does not suffer consequences as a result of his behavior" (National Coalition Against Domestic Violence Organization, 2011).

There is no typical, readily recognized profile of the domestic violence perpetrator or abuser. Those who batter come from every race, background, socioeconomic status, age, and profession in society. However, NCADV has developed some general characteristics of a batterer:

- A batterer objectifies women. He does not see women as people. He does not respect women as a group. Overall, he sees women as property or sexual objects.
- A batterer has low self-esteem and feels powerless and ineffective in the world. He may appear successful but inside he feels inadequate.

- A batterer externalizes the causes of his behavior. He blames his violence on circumstances such as stress, his partner's behavior, a "bad day," alcohol or other factors.
- A batterer may be pleasant and charming between periods of violence, and is often seen as a "nice guy" to outsiders.
- Some behavioral warning signs of a potential batterer include extreme jealousy, possessiveness, a bad temper, unpredictability, cruelty to animals, and verbal abusiveness.

Adapted from National Coalition Against Domestic Violence (2012)
www.ncadv.org

BTC 1B: POWER & CONTROL WHEEL

THE POWER & CONTROL WHEEL

The diagram below shows the relationship of physical abuse to other forms of abuse evident in domestic violence relationships. As you will see, each part of the Power and Control Wheel depicts ways in which abusers control or gain power. You will be able to examine the behaviors abusers use to obtain and maintain control in their relationships. Physical and sexual abuse is only one part of the system of abusive behaviors, as you will see in the diagram below.

Adapted from Ellen Pence and Michael Paymar, *Power and Control: Tactics of Men Who Batter*, Minnesota Program Development, Inc., Duluth, 1986.

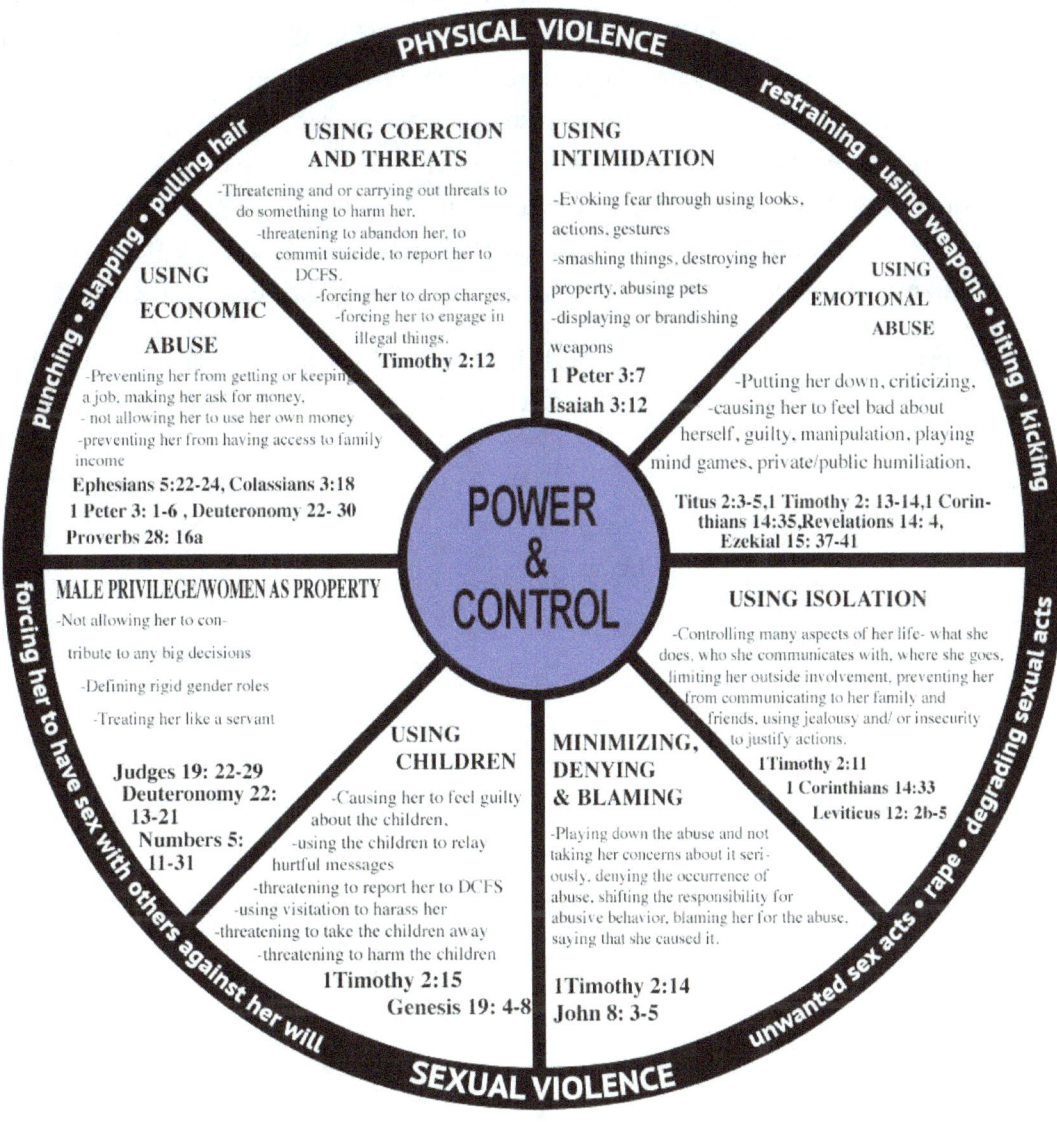

BTC 1B: POWER & CONTROL WHEEL WKST 1

Power and Control Wheel

Vignette #1:

Sherice has been married to Davon for 2 years, and together they have two young children, a 3-year-old boy and a 5-year-old girl. Sherice met Davon in high school, was engaged at 18 and was married at 19. While dating, Davon wanted Sherice to text him every time she went out with friends and required her to check in with him on days that they did not see each other. When Sherice addressed her concern with Davon, he replied, "Baby, I'm just looking out for you. I want to make sure you're safe." Feeling like Davon really cared for her, she obliged with the mandatory texts. Davon's control increased over the years. After they were married, Davon and Sherice moved into an apartment in a city over an hour away from Sherice's family because of a job opportunity for Davon. Sherice stayed at home taking care of the children because Davon said that this was her role, and she was not permitted to leave the house to get a job or attend college. Davon never disclosed how much money there was left over at the end of the month, and would frequently say to Sherice, "men take care of the finances, women take care of the house and children." Feeling like they were each doing their part, Sherice stayed home and would ask Davon for money to purchase items for their children or the house.

Examples of power and control in this relationship: Please write the type of power and control from the wheel and back it up with examples from the vignette:

1. _____
_____
_____
_____

2. _____
_____
_____
_____

3. _____
_____
_____
_____

Vignette #2:

Tierra has been in a relationship with her boyfriend, Marquis, for 7 months. Marquis told Tierra that he was falling in love with her and asked her to move in with him. Feeling like Marquis might be the one for her, Tierra excitedly accepted his invitation and moved in 1 month later. Shortly after moving in with Marquis, Tierra noticed that their relationship was changing. The Marquis who used to compliment her and tell her how beautiful she was, was now constantly putting her down. He commented on her clothing size, stating that "she would never find anyone who loves a fat cow as much as he does," and he often made "mooing" sounds when she was in the room. Marquis overheard Tierra talking to a friend about how she was going to end their relationship. That night Marquis told her that if she left him, she would be sorry that she did and that she'd "better think twice," while making gun gestures with his hand. Immediately after telling her this, Marquis picked up a nearby lamp and threw it across the room and then slammed the door as he left. The next day, Marquis apologized for "losing his cool" and then stated that he loved her and that he would never behave in that way again.

Examples of power and control in this relationship: Please write the type of power and control from the wheel and back it up with examples from the vignette:

1.

2.

3.

Vignette #3:

"My husband and I were high school sweethearts. He had a love for politics, sports, life, and he knew exactly where he was going. We had a perfect marriage—until that first hit. At first, I took his behavior as total love and protection for me. He controlled my every action, my every move—even going to the bathroom. He was an awesome father to my children, but he was unbelievably mean to me. He would often beat me, and one night he raped me. I had wanted to do everything I possibly could to keep my family together for so long. When I finally decided to leave, I wanted to say I had given my marriage my all. I did everything I could and realized that it was not enough. . . . I left even though he threatened to take our children away from me. I knew I had to go when I realized the message I was sending to my children about abuse."—Nia

Examples of power and control in this relationship: Please write the type of power and control from the wheel and back it up with examples from the vignette:

1.

2.

3.

Vignette #4:

Lisa is a 52-year-old married female from a prominent, wealthy Anglo-Protestant family. She had been an active volunteer, working around her husband's schedule and commitments. Behind her facade of perfection, however, lay her misery that resulted from her husband's periodic physical assaults (sometimes resulting in serious bruises) and verbal assaults ("You're fat, ugly, you have no skills and no brains"). She has told no one of her problems, not even her best friend. Because the violence has been well-concealed, and because her husband's power and standing in the community is so strong, she thinks that no one will believe her about the abuse, including a judge. She is frightened to be on her own because she must support herself for the first time in her life. He had always prevented her from working and having financial independence. Other than being a good hostess in the home, Lisa believes she has no occupational skills.

Examples of power and control in this relationship: Please write the type of power and control from the wheel and back it up with examples from the vignette:

1.
_____
_____
_____
_____

2.
_____
_____
_____
_____

3.
_____
_____
_____
_____

Answer Key:

Vignette #1:

1. Isolation: moved away from family; prevented Sherice from leaving the house, under the guise of childcare; preventing her from signing up for online college courses.
2. Economic abuse: not allowing her to know financial details; requiring permission to purchase items
3. Male privilege: making the decisions of the house without her input; stating gender roles for men and women
4. Minimizing/denying/blaming: minimizing her concerns over reporting where she was going

Vignette #2:

1. Emotional abuse: putting Tierra down about her weight; mooing when she was in the room; telling her how much he loved her after threatening (mind games)
2. Intimidation: made gun gestures with his hand; threw a lamp across the room
3. Coercion/threats: told her that she would be sorry for leaving; threatened to harm her if she did

Vignette #3:

1. Physical abuse: hit Nia/ beat her
2. Sexual abuse: raped her
3. Using children: threatened to take away children

Vignette #4:

1. Physical abuse: physical assaults on Lisa sometimes resulting in serious bruises
2. Emotional abuse: telling her she's fat, ugly, and has no skills or brains
3. Economic abuse: preventing her from having a job and financial independence

BTC 2A: CYCLE OF VIOLENCE WHEEL

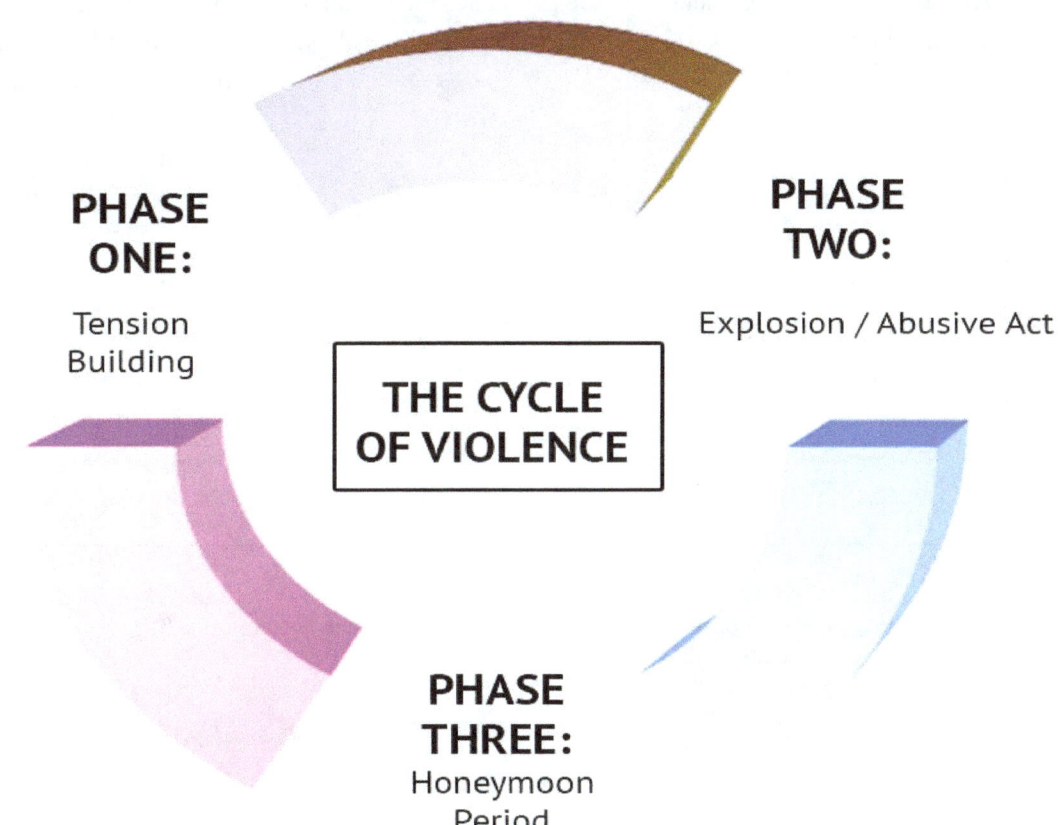

	Phase I	Phase II	Phase III
	Tension begins to mount as the abuser increases threats of violence, often calling the victims names, pushing, or shoving her around.	Abuser is unpredictable; and violence erupts as the abuser throws objects, hits, slaps, kicks, chokes or beats partner with fists; abuses her sexually; or uses weapons such as belts, shoes, sticks, knives, or guns.	Abuser is excessively apologetic, expresses guilt and shame, and promises the violent behavior will never happen again.
	Victim minimizes problems and often will make increasing futile efforts to please the abuser or calm him down.	Victim is helpless; feels trapped, and may also experience denial of the abuser's responsibility for what is occurring.	Abuser appears loving, attentive, and affectionate, often buying gifts for the victim. Victim has mixed feelings.

Phase I	Phase II	Phase III
Abuser increases threats and controls more.	Abuser blames the victim as being the cause of the abuse.	Abuser is manipulative and may minimize the violence or blame the violence on the victim, stating that it never would have happened if the victim hadn't said or done something to make the abuser angry.
Tension becomes intolerable and victim feels as if she is walking on egg shells.	Victim may believe that she is the cause of the abuse.	Victim feels guilty and responsible and often recants and minimizes abuse. Abuser promises change. Victim often considers reconciliation.

Partially adapted from House of Ruth "Intimate Partner Violence Dynamics." 2014
http://www.hruth.org/domestic-violence-dynamics.asp

BTC 2B: CYCLE OF VIOLENCE WORKSHEET 1

Cycle of Violence

Each quote or scenario below represents one of the phases of abuse (Tension, Explosion, and Honeymoon). Take turns reading the quotes below. As a group, we will discuss which phase the quote belongs in and why.

1. "If I can complete all of the housework and have dinner on the table by the time Adam comes home, he should be content. He will have dinner, drink a couple beers and fall asleep watching TV. I just need to keep the kids quiet in their rooms, if they wake him up, Lord only knows what he'll do next."

Phase:_____

_____

_____

_____

_____

2. "I'm terrified. There's broken glass everywhere and I'm scared that me and my children will never be able to be safe. As long as I can keep the attention on myself he will leave the kids alone. I will do whatever it takes to keep him from walking remotely close to their door when he's in a fit of rage. How did I let it get to this point?"

Phase:_____

_____

_____

_____

_____

3. "Adam came home with a brand new vase to replace the one he broke last night. That must mean he realizes what he did and he has to change now that he is aware of what his anger does to us—to his family. We've been together for 5 years, there's no way I can leave him now. Maybe things will change, maybe I can change him."

Phase:_____

_____

_____

_____

_____

4. "I went into the house and saw him in the kitchen. He was looking for something to eat. It was apparent that he was in a bad mood, slamming cabinet doors and cursing to himself. 'How come there isn't any food in the house?!' he shouted. I had to tread carefully, and make sure I chose the right words. At that moment, I knew that anything I said could set him off."

Phase:_____

_____

_____

_____

_____

5. "We met at a dance and almost immediately we became inseparable. He was cute and funny and seemed to not be able to get enough of me. After 15 years of a man who did not seem to like me much this was a refreshing situation. He called and dropped by with flowers and was just so charming. He even seemed to get along with my sons, who at that time were early teens and hard to get along with. I knew he had just gotten out of prison, but as he always said, he had learned his lesson. I should have seen the warning signs right then and there but I did not.

He moved in rather quickly, I just love to do things fast, and things seemed so blissful. He made coffee in the morning and cleaned up after himself and just could not get enough of the togetherness I had been craving. The abuse did not start out physical, it started with: I was lucky to have him, he could do so much better than me, the house needed to be cleaner, the boys needed to be quieter, and I needed to be home with him when he was, that my friends were not really my friends, and on and on.

The first sign of the physical abuse started not with hitting but pushing and grabbing. First came the apologies: 'I am so sorry I did not mean to grab you so hard but if you had only listened or did something right the first time we would have not had to go through that fight.' As time went on, the abuse got worse and happened at a faster pace. He started punching and kicking and burning and cutting. I was hiding all this from people who loved me, so I had no one to turn to."

Phase:_____

_____
_____
_____
_____

6. "I woke up the next morning, my body bruised from several harsh blows. I looked in the mirror to see a purple ring around my right eye. Last night was a disaster. I had come home late last night after work. That didn't sit well with my husband. I walked into the kitchen and found a bouquet of roses perched in the center of the kitchen table. Beside the bouquet was a beautiful card. It read, 'I'm sorry, and I love you.' I sighed, same as usual. I guess he's going to be sweet to me today, let's see how it is tomorrow."

Phase:_____

_____
_____
_____
_____

BTC 3A: EQUALITY WHEEL

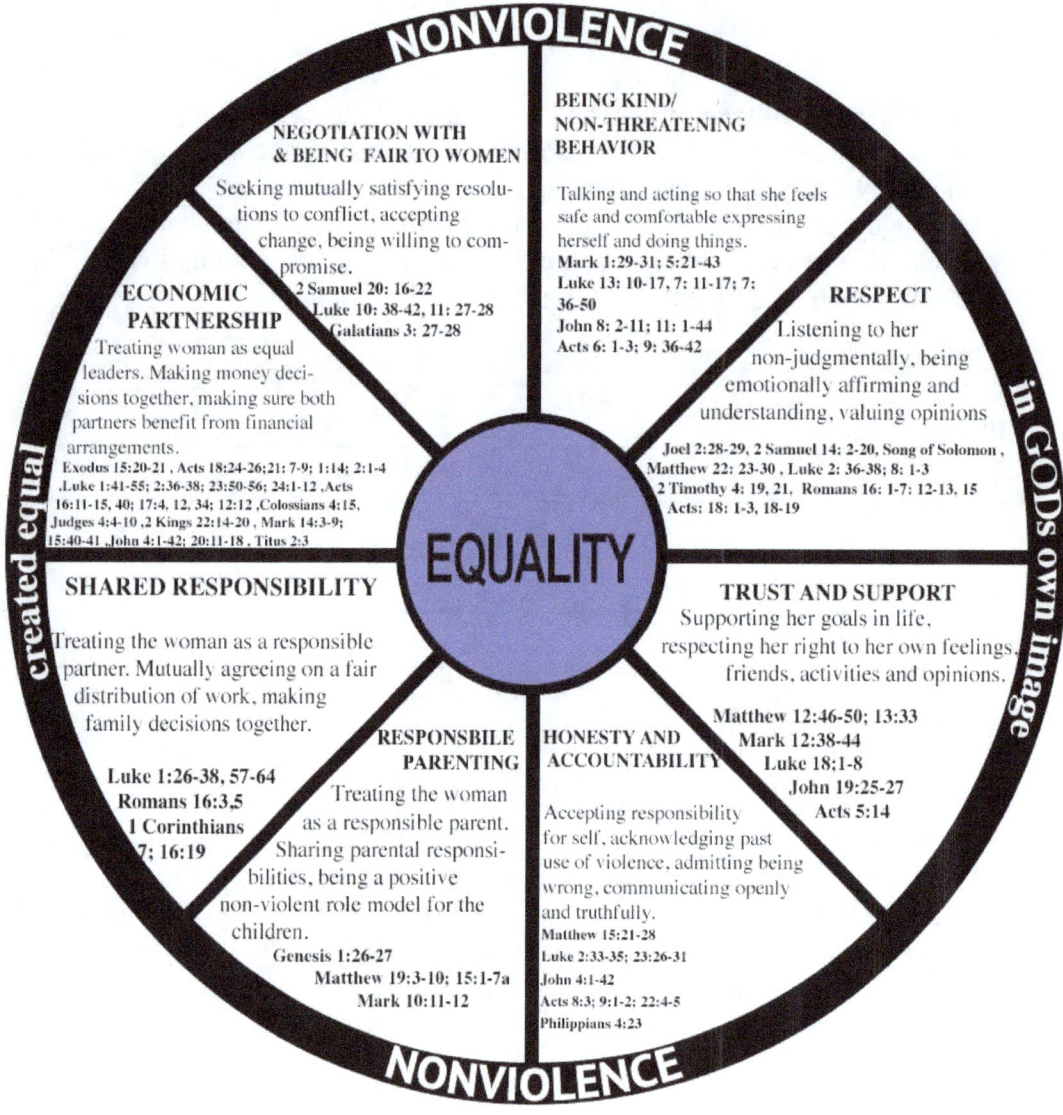

Partially adapted from: Ellen Pence and Michael Paymar, *Equality Wheel*, Minnesota Program Development, Inc., Duluth, 1986.

What Does The Bible Have To Say About…

Verbal Abuse: Scripture reveals to us that the words we speak can be considered a form of violence.

Ephesians 4:29: "Let no corrupt communication proceed out of your mouth, but that which is good to the use of edifying, that it may minister grace unto the hearers."

James 1:26: "If any man among you seem to be religious, and bridleth not his tongue, but deceiveth his own heart, this man's religion is vain."

James 3:10: "Out of the same mouth proceedeth blessing and cursing. My brethren, these things ought not be so."

Ephesians 4:31: "Let all bitterness, and wrath and anger and clamour and evil speaking be put away from you, with all malice."

Proverbs 10:6: "Blessings are upon the head of the just; but violence covereth the mouth of the wicked."

Proverbs 10:11: "The mouth of a righteous man is a well of life: but violence covereth the mouth of the wicked."

Colossians 3: 8: "But now ye also put off all these: anger, wrath, malice, blasphemy, filthy communication out of your mouth."

The Bible Condemns Violence: Many passages in the Bible speak out on the issue of violence and reveal God's attitude toward those that repeatedly use violence.

Zephaniah 1:9: "In the same day also will I punish all those that leap on the threshold, which fill their masters' houses with violence and deceit."

Psalm 11:5: "The Lord trieth the righteous: but the wicked and him that loveth violence his soul hateth."

Malachi 2:16-17: "I hate […] a man's covering his wife with violence, as well as with his garment." Says the Lord Almighty…"? You have wearied the Lord with your words…."

James 1:19, 20: "Wherefore, my beloved brethren, let every man be swift to hear, slow to speak, slow to wrath: For the wrath of the man worketh not the righteousness of God."

The Responsibility of the Church to Hold Abusers Accountable: Religious leaders are encouraged to hold their fellow believers accountable by showing a sinning Brother or Sister the error of their ways. In the Old Testament, those who had a position of being the spiritual guides of God's people likewise had an obligation to warn those who were doing wrong of the consequences that would ensue if they did not change their ways.

Romans 15:14: "And I myself also am persuaded of you, my brethren, that ye also are full of goodness, filled with all knowledge, able also to admonish one another."

James 5:19, 20: "Brethren, if any of you do err from the truth, and one convert him; Let him know, that he which converteth the sinner from the error of his way shall save a soul from death, and shall hide a multitude of sins."

Men in Healthy Relationships

Colossians 3:19: "Husbands, love your wives, and be not bitter against them."

1 Timothy 3:2: "Therefore an overseer must be above reproach, the husband of one wife, sober-minded, self-controlled, respectable, hospitable, and able to teach."

Ephesians 5:25: "Husbands love your wife, even as Christ also loved the church and gave himself for it."

Ephesians 5:33: "Nevertheless let every one of you in particular so love his wife as himself; and the wife see that she reverence her husband."

Colossians 3:21: "Fathers, provoke not your children to anger, lest they be discouraged."

Ephesians 5:3-5: "For this ye know, that no whoremonger, nor unclean person, nor covetous man, who is an idolater, hath any inheritance in the kingdom of Christ and of God."

Women in Healthy Relationships

Colossians 3:18: "Wives, submit yourselves unto your own husbands, as it is fit in the Lord."

Partnership

Ephesians 5:31: "For this cause shall a man leave his father and mother and shall be joined unto his wife and they two shall be one flesh."

Children

Colossians 3:20: "Children, obey your parents in all things: for this is well pleasing unto the Lord."

1 John 3:18: "My little children, let us not love in word, neither in tongue; but in deed and in truth."

Living In Abuse

2 Thessalonians 3:6: "Now we command you…in the name of our Lord Jesus Christ, that ye withdraw yourselves from every brother that walketh disorderly, and not after the traditions which he received of us."

Equally Yoked

Mark 3:25: "If a house is divided against itself, that house cannot stand."

2 Corinthians 6:14-15: "Do not be yoked together with unbelievers. For what do righteousness and wickedness have in common? Or what fellowship can light have with darkness?"

BTC 3B: HEALTHY RELATIONSHIP ARTICLE

Jonathan Aigner and Kelsey Seifert: "I was raised as a Southern Baptist homeschooler deep in the heart of Texas."

By Jenny Rae Armstrong on February 11, 2013 in equally yoked

I first stumbled across Jonathan Aigner's writing in an article he wrote for Mutuality. I was struck by his ability to express his points clearly and simply, without sacrificing the personal elements that make his story so compelling. I'm thrilled to have him blogging for Equally Yoked today, and hope you enjoy his post as much as I do!

Egalitarian is a bad word where I'm from. Actually, it's a concept so foreign to the people I grew up with, I usually have to explain it, and then it becomes a bad word.

See, I was raised as a Southern Baptist homeschooler deep in the heart of Texas, where we like our steaks rare, our trucks big, and our women in their place. Patriarchy dominated our homes, our preaching, our homeschooling conferences. It was an essential doctrine, right next to the virgin birth and bodily resurrection.

Things changed for me during grad school in the far away land of Illinois. By the time I married my strong, capable, beautiful wife, I was an egalitarian, at least theoretically.

Many of my complementarian friends are constantly preoccupied with how to best contort themselves into being good stereotypical husbands and wives. The men labor under the crushing weight of having to always be protectors, providers, and priests. The women allow their own unique gifts and sense of calling to be buried in the name of being a "cheerful helpmeet." Sadly, individuality is far too often lost in the name of "biblical" manhood and womanhood.

Thankfully, that's not been my experience. It isn't always easy. Old habits die hard and hierarchical roots run deep, but I'm finding egalitarian marriage to be increasingly natural.

Here are the things I appreciate most about being "equally yoked."

We fulfill functions, not roles.

Of course, we're still male and female as God created us, but our gender doesn't predestine how our relationship is going to work itself out. We both provide. We both protect. We both lead spiritually. We both do housework. We both lead and we both submit. Sometimes it's decided by our particular strengths. Other times it's decided by our circumstances. The one constant is that we both are willing to step up whenever and wherever we're needed. After all, reducing someone's entire existence to a set of rules is more than just stereotyping, it's dehumanizing.

We discover each other anew every day.

We are better able to understand each other because we don't assume anything. We don't assume that I have blue ears and she has pink. Neither of us fit into these traditional stereotypes, and I don't think we can ever really get to know each other if we boil manhood and womanhood down that way. It's deeply honoring to have a spouse that really seeks to understand you. We approach each other as mysteries to be discovered and that makes life endlessly exciting and love endlessly regenerating.

We don't have to play silly "gender" games.

A friend once cautioned Kelsey not to take on too many home maintenance tasks, since that sort of thing was supposed to be my responsibility. Such a concept was hilarious to us, since Kelsey is much better at working with her hands than I am. She doesn't have to tiptoe around, taking great care not to bruise my fragile male ego. On the other hand, of the two of us, I'm better in the kitchen, and that isn't at all threatening to Kelsey's sense of self-worth.

Being equal means we just don't have to worry about all that stuff.

We collaborate in planning our life direction.

I'm sharpened by a wife who is free to take me to task over my decisions and motivations. She can push back when she disagrees without worrying that I'm going to meltdown into a "manly" temper tantrum or throw my weight around. When we disagree, we talk about it. I recently saw a video produced by a hierarchical organization that said husbands should "dominate in all areas of eternal significance," especially in marriage and family. I think that's a grave error. It's a real joy for us to work together in figuring out our next steps.

We learn how to really listen and understand.

Most complementarians don't get how egalitarians settle differences. How we listen to each other when we disagree, trying to find the core of the concern. How we don't pressure issues and take time – sometimes months or years to be prayerful and understanding. How we never use power plays to convince or coerce the other. Nobody has a veto. Nobody has the final word. We just pray and listen to each other till we agree.

We've learned we really don't disagree very much and when we do there is usually growing we both need to do. If we don't agree we just aren't done talking, understanding and praying. Marrying a counselor definitely helps in this area, but I suspect this kind of communication is common within egalitarian marriages.

We have a deep and fun friendship.

Because we are constantly growing together, we really prefer to spend time together than with anyone else. In fact, we have to remind ourselves to schedule time with friends. We uncover new ways of having fun and can laugh at ourselves and each other because of the safe vulnerability between us.

I don't always have to be the strong one.

Either one of us can be strong when the other one is weak.

I married a strong person. She's not intimidated by anyone. In fact, on multiple occasions I've seen Kelsey's natural confidence intimidate the most brazenly egotistical of men. I used to feel threatened by strong women, but I've found it to be a great source of comfort in our marriage, particularly during the times I've struggled most. In a lot of hierarchical marriages, I've seen men treat their wives as if they were not quite adults. But I have a full partner who is quite capable of helping me, even carrying me, through the darkest times.

We are one, but we are still two.

This is where I've found the redemptive message of mutuality to be most life-giving. We aren't some strange amalgamation of Kelsey and Jonathan (Kelsathan?). We're still Kelsey and Jonathan.

Sometimes I think my complementarian friends are just watching us, waiting for the bottom to fall out. They see us, a male elementary music teacher married to a professional, independent woman with a different last name, and they seem to be skeptical that we can function so well. I tell them that it's easier. It's easier when we're both free to be ourselves, manifesting unique set of gifts, inclinations, and abilities. I think it makes for a much more dynamic relationship.

After all, I'm convinced that the paradigms of "biblical" manhood and womanhood are fabrications. The highest calling of any person is to follow Christ wholeheartedly. A marriage relationship free of gender rigidity has given me the freedom to do so.

See more at: http://www.jennyraearmstrong.com/2013/02/11/jonathan-aigner-and-kelsey-seifert-i-was-raised-as-a-southern-baptist-homeschooler-deep-in-the-heart-of-texas-where-we-like-our-steaks-rare-our-trucks-big-and-our-women-in-their-place/#sthash.8t0XqEGN.dpuf

Included with permission from the author, Jenny Rae Armstrong

UTV 1: Self Reflections

Why I Stayed

There are many different reasons why women stay in abusive relationships. This is MY story…

My reasons for staying were:

_____
_____
_____
_____

My thoughts for staying were:

_____
_____
_____
_____

These people thought:

My family

_____
_____
_____
_____

My friends

_____
_____
_____
_____

My children

_____
_____
_____
_____

What I feared most was:

_____
_____
_____
_____

What it took for me to leave was:

_____
_____
_____
_____

UTV 2A: REASONS WHY

REASONS WHY SHE STAYS

People who have not experienced abuse by an intimate partner often maintain that they if their partner abused them they would instantly leave the relationship. However, remaining in or leaving an abusive relationship is a complex decision that may serve as a very rational survival mechanism. Domestic violence represents a serious violent crime, and there are many emotional, physical, financial, social, and spiritual obstacles to overcome in leaving an abusive relationship. The following is an abbreviated list of some reasons victims of abuse often choose to stay in or return to an abusive relationship.

- Denial/excuses: A DV survivor may find it difficult to classify herself as abused or battered, and deny that there is a problem. Victims may believe the abusers excuses to justify the violence, i.e., job stress, substance abuse
- Traumatic bonding: When the person who is isolating, abusing, and dehumanizing the victim is the same person providing her with the basics needed for survival (i.e., food, shelter, or some pain relief or affection) a form of traumatic bonding can occur, which leads to an irrational feeling of bonding to the abuser, and this feeling of being traumatically bonded is often mistaken for love. The victim may lose her own beliefs and identity and identify with her abuser.
- Guilt/self-blame: The victim may believe that the abuse is her fault, that she provoked it and deserves it. Victims may also believe that abuse is an unavoidable part of their lives.
- Spiritual/religious, distorted religious beliefs and misguided teachings: Such beliefs may lead victims to think they have to tolerate the abuse to show their adherence to the faith.
- Family pressure: Pressure by those who either believe that there is no excuse for leaving a marriage or have been deceived into denial by the abusers charismatic behavior.
- Cultural and racial defenses and stereotypes: These may be cited by offenders, victims, and other community members who may not be cognizant that although domestic violence occurs among all races, no excuses, save self-defense, ever justifies the abuse.
- Fear of retaliation or reprisal/belief of abuser's threats to kill her and her children if she attempts to leave: It is estimated that a battered woman is 75%t more likely to be murdered when she tries to flee or has fled than when she stays. It is dangerous for counsel to advise a victim simply to leave without ensuring that a trained advocate or attorney has worked with her to conduct extensive safety planning.
- Fear of losing child custody: This fear can immobilize even the most determined abuse victim. Abusers frequently use threats of obtaining custody to exact agreement to their liking.
- Gratitude toward the abuser because he has helped support and raise her children from a previous relationship: Additionally, a victim who is obese, has mental health, medical or other

serious problems, or is illiterate often appreciates that the abuser professes his love, despite the victim's perceived faults. Through constant psychological abuse many abusers fuel the victim's low self-esteem and reinforce her belief that she deserves no better than an abusive partner.

- No place to go/fear of homelessness/financial abuse/ Victim may feel that she has no other place to turn to for money, shelter, support, etc.
- Keeping the family unit together; children's best interest: Some survivors believe it is in the children's best interest to have both parents in the home. The victims-as well as their counsel, may be unaware of the traumatic impact of children witnessing domestic violence, whether or not they have been beaten by the abuser.
- Love/ Hope for the violence to stop
- Cultural values and beliefs/ Racial Loyalty: There may be cultural pressures to stay. For instance, many African American women may subscribe to the belief that they must be strong (pride) deny violence, deny vulnerability; psycho-cultural implications exist for Black women who have internalized the notion that they must remain unwaveringly strong in the face of all adversity (Bell & Mattis, 2000). In subscribing to **Racial Loyalty**, many African American women in domestic violence relationships must confront a racial ideology that tends to accuse abused woman of betraying their race in those instances when they opt to report their victimization to the police or other formal public authority (Few, 2000). Crenshaw (2000) described this oppressive racial loyalty as an ingrained feature of the racialized social reality of African American abused women.
- Religious views: God will take care of it; pray; the Lord will change him.
- Socialized to sacrifice: Research shows that many African American females are generally socialized to sacrifice their individual desires for the integration and survival of the family unit within society, thus Black women who are abused must often choose between survival of their family and survival of themselves as healthy whole individuals (Billingsley, 1992). "The African American woman may withstand abuse and make a conscious self-sacrifice for what she perceives as the greater good of the community but to her own physical, psychological and spiritual detriment" (Bent-Goodley, 2001, p. 323).

Partially adapted from Buel, S.M.,(1999). Fifty Obstacles to Leaving, a.k.a., Why Abuse Victims Stay. *The Colorado Lawyer* (28) 10-19

UTV 2B: REASONS WHY WORKSHEET 1

Why Does She Stay Worksheet

Dialogue #1

Milvia (DV Victim): Jerard was really upset last night. He came home from work and something was wrong. I could just tell. He came into the kitchen while I was making dinner. I was almost finished, just waiting for the chicken to finish baking in the oven. I guess he wanted dinner as soon as he got home because he started throwing the plates against the wall. He picked up a boiling pot of water and threw it at me.

Jenna (Friend): Are you OK? Did you get burned?!

Milvia (DV Victim) : I moved out of the way just in time. Some water splashed on my foot but I was still wearing shoes, so I didn't get burned.

Jenna (Friend): You have got to leave, next time it might be your face! I'm worried about you.

Milvia (DV Victim): Jerard was just having a stressful day at work, he doesn't come home and behave like that usually. If I had dinner ready on time, this situation would have never occurred.

Jenna (Friend): You deserve to be treated better than this, Milvia. It's not okay that you're going through this.

Milvia (DV Victim): I know he doesn't mean it. I love him, Kristen, and I have to do what is necessary to keep my marriage together. You know my faith doesn't want me to practice divorce.

Why is Milvia staying?

1._____
_____
_____
_____

2._____
_____
_____
_____

3._____
_____
_____
_____

Why is Melissa staying?

1._____
_____
_____
_____
_____

2._____
_____
_____
_____
_____

3._____
_____
_____
_____

Dialogue #2:

Tarvia (friend): It's summer and you're wearing long sleeves! Are you feeling okay?

Denice (DV Victim): Yeah, I'm OK. You know the valley gets cold in the evenings Tarvia.

Tarvia (friend): You're hiding something, I know you too well. Did he hit you again?

Denice (DV Victim): We…had an argument last night. He doesn't want to spend Thanksgiving with my family this year. I disagreed; you know I don't see my mom very often. He flipped. He grabbed my arms as I tried to walk away and then threw me on the coffee table.

Tarvia (friend): Will you please come stay with me? You could've been hurt.

Denice (DV Victim): I can't leave. I don't want my family to know what's going on. Maybe he'll agree to go to anger management classes or counseling. You know he was abused growing up, I don't think he can help it. He's not a monster.

Tarvia (friend): I don't know. It keeps happening, and every time is worse than before. I'm scared for your life, friend.

Denice (DV Victim): I know you are. But if I leave instead of trying to get him help, he may come after me and then what do I do? I don't think I can survive financially without him. LA is expensive, and I haven't worked in several years.

Why is Denice staying?

1. _____
_____
_____
_____

2. _____
_____
_____
_____

3. _____
_____
_____
_____

Dialogue #3:

Rita (Mother): I can never get in contact with you anymore. It's been a year since we've spoken. Ever since you got into a relationship with Brian, you've been so distant from me. I can't believe you moved all the way to Texas, when your family is here in California.

Yvette (DV Victim): I'm sorry mom. I should never have moved so far away and left everyone behind. I miss you, and my sisters. I really do want to call you more often, it's just so hard sometimes....

Rita (Mother): What's hard about just picking up the phone and calling me? Don't you know I want to hear from you? I worry about you.

Yvette (DV Victim): You don't understand mom. I'm not allowed to contact anyone! Not you, not my friends, not anyone! It's a risk talking to you right now. If Brian finds out, I know he'll hurt me again.

Rita (Mother): Oh my goodness, I can't believe this is happening to you! You have to leave him! He's taking you away from your family!

Yvette (DV Victim): I know, but he tells me all the time that he's the only family I need. He said if I really love him, I wouldn't need anyone else but him. I do love him, so I try to do what he says. But, then when I am alone with him, he beats me. It just doesn't make sense. Before I moved to Texas, he never laid a finger on me. Now that I have no one around me, he's become this monster!

Rita (Mother): Please come back home, honey, you're not safe over there.

Yvette (DV Victim): I want to so bad mom, but I can't. I have no money, and no means of transportation. As soon as I moved to Texas with him last year, he never let me work. He also took all the money that I had, so that I would have to ask him for money whenever I needed something. There's nothing I can do but keep believing that things will get better. I am certain that if I try to leave, it could get much worse than it is now.

Why is Yvette staying?

1._____
_____
_____
_____

2._____
_____
_____
_____

3._____
_____
_____
_____

Dialogue #4:

Malia (friend): What's with the sun glasses in the house? There's not sunlight in here. (Malia reaches towards Alenia and remove's Alenika sunglasses, as Alenika gasps in horror.)

Alenika (DV Victim): I didn't want you to see my bruises.

Malia (friend): That lunatic! I can't believe he hit you. Are you OK? I knew Allen was crazy from the moment I first saw him!

Alenika (DV Victim): It's OK, it's really not that bad. I'm fine. He was just a little angry when I got home late from work. He promised me that he won't hit me again. Besides, I am partly to blame…I was 15 minutes late when I got home!

Malia (friend): Are you seriously blaming yourself for Allen's abusiveness? You seriously need to leave him, girl! Alenika, come stay with me. I can help you get a restraining order against him. I'll help you through this.

Alenika (DV Victim): Thank you Malia, but I can't leave. We have two children together, and he always tells me that if I left him…he would take my babies away from me. I can't live without my children. I need my family to be together no matter what. Please don't worry about me. Like I said, it's not that bad. Everything is going to be OK.

Why is Alenika staying?

1. _____
_____
_____
_____

2. _____
_____
_____
_____

3. _____
_____
_____
_____

Answer Key:

Dialogue #1:

1. Denial
2. Hope for Change
3. Love
4. Religious pressure
5. Believes the myths about domestic violence

Dialogue #2:

1. Economic dependence
2. Danger of leaving
3. Isolation
4. Pressure to be nurturing
5. Shame/embarrassment

Dialogue #3

1. Social isolation
2. Economic dependence
3. Fear of leaving
4. Hope for violence to cease
5. Love for the perpetrator

Dialogue #4

1. Denial about the abuse
2. Fear of losing children
3. Keeping the family together
4. Hope for change
5. Guilt/ self blame

UTV 3A: SAFETY PLANNING

Safety Planning Checklist

PREPARING TO LEAVE:

If you are in an abusive relationship and preparing to leave, here is a checklist of important safety precautions you can take.

- ✓ Keep all evidence of physical violence, such as photographs, medical records, etc.
- ✓ Document all violent incidences, with dates, times, locations, and threats made.
- ✓ Inform trusted friends or neighbors about the situation and alert them to call the police if they here violent noises.
- ✓ Set aside emergency money, or have trusted friends /family hold money for you.
- ✓ Contact local battered woman's shelter and find out about resources available to you.
- ✓ Preprogram emergency numbers into the telephone, including 911.

BREAKING FREE:

- ✓ Consider your option to request a police escort while you leave.
- ✓ Devise a plan for how and where you will escape.
- ✓ Set aside emergency money.
- ✓ Hide an extra set of car keys.
- ✓ Bring all important phone numbers of friends, relatives, doctors, schools, etc.
- ✓ Take important items with you, such as; driver's license, passport, green card, work permit, birth certificate, medicine, checkbooks, credit cards, welfare identification, car registration and insurance information, children's school records, immunization records, medical records, address book, divorce papers, custody orders, other legal documents, unpaid bills, extra clothing, money, keys to car, house and work, and valued personal possessions.
- ✓ Develop false trails

SAFTEY PRECAUTIONS IN THE AFTERMATH:

- ✓ **If obtaining a restraining order and abuser leaves:** Change locks and phone number and request for your phone company to implement Caller Id.
- ✓ Install security system, smoke alarms, and an outside motion sensitive lighting system.
- ✓ Notify neighbors about the restraining order and ask them to call police immediately if they see the abuser near the home.

- ✓ Give copies of restraining order to employers, neighbors and schools along with picture of the perpetrator.
- ✓ Tell those who care for your children, make sure they know those who have authorization to pick up the kid and give them copies of restraining order.
- ✓ Avoid bank stores and other places that you frequented when living with the offender.
- ✓ Notify work and try to arrange for your calls to be screened.
- ✓ Report abuse of a restraining order immediately, even if it seems harmless, such as a telephone call or letter.
- ✓ **If you leave the home:** Consider changing work route and work hours.
- ✓ Consider renting a P.O. Box
- ✓ Avoid banks, stores and areas that you frequented when living with abuser.
- ✓ Reschedule appointments that the abuser is aware of.
- ✓ Be mindful who you give your new address and phone number to.

Adapted from: The National Center for Victims of Crime (1998)
http://www.victimsofcrime.org

Superior Court orders for relief:

As a DV survivor you have the right to go to the Superior Court and file a petition requesting orders for relief. The court can order a restrained person the following:

- ✓ Orders restraining the attacker from abusing victim and other family members
- ✓ Not to have a gun or ammunition
- ✓ Directing attacker to leave household
- ✓ Directing the offender to obey child custody and visitation orders
- ✓ Preventing the attacker from entering the residence, school, business, or place of employment of the victim
- ✓ Directing the attacker to pay child and/ or spousal support
- ✓ Restraining the attacker from molesting or interfering with minor children in the custody of the victim
    - o Understand that any violation of a restraining order is a crime.

Adapted from The Superior Court of California County of Orange
http://www.occourts.org/self-help/restrainingorders/domesticviolence.html

UTV 3B: THINKING ABOUT LEAVING

Thinking About Leaving My Abuser

1. Where to go?

    - Stay with a friend or relatives
    - Avoid staying with a man unless he is a relative.
      (Living with a man you are not married to could hurt you chances of getting custody of your children and spousal support.)
    - Go to a battered women's shelter with your children. There you can obtain help regarding legal and financial resources from the staff as well as counseling, emotional support, and advocacy for you and your children
    - You can call 211 for listings of domestic violence shelters and programs
    - Contact the police immediately if you or your children are in immediate danger. Temporary protective custody may then be arranged. Permanent custody will be decided later by a judge.

2. Can my children leave with me?

    - Yes you can, if you can do this safely.
    - It is imperative that you get legal custody within a few days.
    - If you do not have your children with you, it may be difficulty filing for temporary custody of your children. The parent who has the physical possession of the children may have an advantage getting temporary custody.
    - Your partner may attempt to kidnap or harm the children to get you to return. Call 911 if in immediate danger.

    Adapted from: Domestic Violence Organization
    http://www.domesticviolence.org/questions-about-leaving/

EA 1: MYTHS ABOUT ABUSERS

Myths about Abusers

Myth: Alcohol causes battering. People who batter are alcoholics.
Fact: Very often, drinking and battering do go together, and alcohol accelerates the battering problem. But drinking does NOT cause battering. Drinking may allow someone to let down his or her inhibitions and become violent. Someone who drinks and is violent can learn to control both of these behaviors, and get help to do so.

Myth: Once a batterer, always a batterer.
Fact: Although the prognosis for change is dim some men do stop their violent behavior. Men have more success at stopping physical violence than they do at stopping verbal and emotional violence. It is estimated that it will take between 3 and 5 years of weekly therapy for a man to make a significant, lasting change in all aspects of his violent behavior.

Myth: "I just lost it."
Fact: Batterers say they could not help themselves from using violence. Most men who batter use other methods of dealing with frustration, anger or "provocation" when it is convenient for them. When the batterer feels angry, he does not beat up his boss, his secretary, the neighbor, a stranger on the street, or children playing in the next yard. Only in the privacy of his own home or when he perceives he will receive no negative consequences will he choose to use violence toward his female partner and possibly his children. In the vast majority of cases, he will batter no one else

When the perpetrator uses violence, it is because he has made an assessment of the situation and has determined that:

- What I am doing is not wrong.
- If it is wrong, I will not get caught.
- If I get caught, I can talk my way out.
- If I cannot talk my way out, the penalties will be minor. I will decide what the penalties are.

In these "I just lost it" episodes of violence, batterers say and do things they know will hurt their victim. They yell obscenities and threats. They kick pregnant women in the stomach. They hit the victim in places that will be seen or hidden, depending on the message they want to be delivered by the violence. Batterers use violence because they know they can and no one will stop them or apply negative consequences.

Myth: Abusers batter because they have low self-esteem.

Fact: Many people believe that batterers are violent because they feel bad about themselves. They pick on their partners to make themselves feel better. While it may be true that many or all batterers have low self-esteem, this does not explain why they batter. There are many men and women with low self-esteem who are not violent.

Myth: Batterers are mentally ill.
Fact: It is worth noting that in an extremely small percentage of cases, violent behavior may stem from a brain disorder or damage. However, people with this condition commit violent acts at random toward those with whom they're in contact. This is not the case in the vast majority of battering relationships. While some batterers use such excuses as physical problems, drinking, and war flashbacks to justify their actions, these "afflictions" usually do not cause them to harm anyone else except their partners. Battering is not a disease but rather a learned behavior. Abusive behavior is within a person's control. A person uses violence to obtain and maintain control over another person. More importantly, battering can be lethal; it is a deadly crime that can be perpetuated by social institutions unless they intervene to stop it.

Myth: He was abused as a child and needs therapy for it.
Fact: Multiple research studies have examined the question of whether men who abuse women tend to be survivors of childhood abuse, and the link has turned out to be weak. A bad childhood doesn't cause a man to become an abuser, but it can contribute to making a man who is abusive especially dangerous. For some abusive men, the blame-the-childhood approach has an additional reason for being appealing: By focusing on what his mother did wrong, he gets to blame a woman for his mistreatment of women. This explanation can also appeal to the abused woman herself, since it makes sense out of his behavior and gives her someone safe to be angry at, since getting angry at him always seems to blow up in her face. The abuser only wants to draw attention to his terrible childhood if it's an excuse to stay the same, not if it's a reason to change. (*Why Does He Do That?* by Lundy Bancroft).

Myth: He is abusive because he feels so strongly for me.
Fact: Most abusive men have close relationships with people other than their wives or girlfriends. My clients may feel deep fondness for one or both of their parents, a sibling, a dear friend, an aunt or uncle. Do they abuse their other loved ones? Rarely. It isn't the love or deep affection that causes his behavior problem. (*Why Does He Do That?* by Lundy Bancroft).

Adapted from Safe Haven Shelter Organization (2013)
http://www.safehavenshelter.org/myths-about-abusers/

Characteristics of Abusive Men

1. **Pressure**: Pressures you to commit to an exclusive relationship too quickly.

2. **Possessiveness**: Extremely jealous and excessively possessive and is threatened by your relationship with your friends and/or family. Some other indicators include- Frequently calls to determine your whereabouts and if you are with someone else, accusations of unfaithfulness.

3. **Controlling**: Frequently checks your phone and email and closely monitors your chargers. Limits your visits to friends and family members. Interrogates you regarding who you're whereabouts and who you spend your time with. Restricts phone calls. Discourages you from attending school, church or social events. Controls the money and requires that you ask permission before going anywhere. May dictate your clothing attire, and everything pertaining to appearance, including hair style and cosmetics.

4. **Unrealistic expectations**: Holds unrealistic standards and demands that you meet his every need.

5. **Isolation**: Tries to isolate you from your family and friends so you are easier to control. Accuses your friends of being against him. Will be threatened by your holding a job, since you might meet other men there, and since it may decrease your economic dependence on him.

6. **Blames others for his problems or mistakes**: Shifts the responsibility onto others for his actions.

7. **Makes others responsible for his feelings**: Feels that other people are responsible for his feelings and does not see his contribution to his own feelings.

8. **Hypersensitivity**: Is overly sensitive and "personalizes" things which contributes to paranoid nature of thinking that you are purposefully doing things to upset him.

9. **Force during sex or play fighting**: Is inappropriately physically aggressive at times.

10. **Verbal abuse**: Is overly critical of you, ridicules and negatively labels you and often highlights areas where you are more insecure (weight, parenting, intelligence, etc.). May humiliate and embarrass you in front of your friends or family. Uses manipulation, and plays mind games.

11. **Inflexible sex-roles**: Treats you like a subordinate. Expects to be the one to tell you what each of you should be doing. Expects complete and immediate obedience.

12. **Rapid mood swings**: Abrupt, shifting mood swings: for example, calm and affectionate one moment and angry and distant the next. May drive his vehicle in an intimidating manner to frighten you when he is angry. May strike out at things or throw objects and then minimize his actions.

13. **History of battering**: Admits that he has been abusive with past partners but says that they deserved this or provoked the abuse.

14. **Threats of violence**: Makes statements that he will kill you or threatens you and then dismisses it as no big deal when he is confronted. Minimizes or denies that he has made these statements.

Adapted from Domestic Violence Organization
http://www.domesticviolence.org/who-are-the-abusers/

EA 2A: CHARACTERISTICS WORKSHEET

Characteristics of Abusive Men

Vignette #1: Kara

I met Daniel at a friend's birthday party. He was charming, funny, and very attractive. I knew after talking to him that I wanted to go out and see if we had a connection. I was so excited when he asked for my number and if he could take me out! We went out on a couple dates, and I could tell there was something different about him, and I was intrigued. Daniel said that he had never felt this comfortable with anyone. He said he could trust me, and after three dates, he asked me to be his girlfriend, because he couldn't imagine spending his time with anyone else. About a month after we started our relationship I began to see differences. We were out eating dinner one night, and he became so upset. One of the servers tripped, and someone else's drink spilled on his new shirt. He made a scene in the restaurant, yelling at the server and talking to the manager about what happened. See, the funny thing was that he tripped the server with his chair when he was getting up. It wasn't the server's fault but it was like he was oblivious to what he did. I was embarrassed. On the drive home, I tried to explain the part he had in the incident but it only made him angrier. He said that I was taking the server's side and that I didn't care about his feelings or his ruined shirt. He called the server incompetent and said that maybe my boss was right in calling me incompetent, since I didn't see his point of view. I didn't want to say anything else, because, clearly, he was not going to listen to me, and I didn't want to argue. I was hurt by his comment, because I just received a low performance evaluation at work and was put on an action plan. I was scared of losing my only source of income and was doubting my abilities at work. How could he use what I told him in confidence against me like that? Over a stain on a shirt? We sat in silence on the car ride home and I wondered how he would be when it came to issues that were actually important.

Examples of characteristics of abusive men: Write the characteristic displayed and back it up with examples from the vignette:

1. _____
_____
_____

2. _____
_____
_____

3. _____
_____
_____

Vignette #2: Alexis

I have been with Carlos for 3 years, and we have a 3-month-old son, Manuel. I'm a stay-at-home mom because daycare is expensive, and it would take my whole paycheck to afford it. I enjoy the one-on-one time with my son; however, Carlos has changed his behavior drastically since our son was born. He expects me to fulfill the same roles as I did pre-baby: keep the house clean, cook all of the meals, and spend time with him every evening. The baby keeps me busy, waking up constantly to be fed or changed. Carlos doesn't seem to understand. He doesn't want to see piles of laundry, the trash needing to be taken out, or even some dust on the TV stand. Everything needs to be spotless in the house, and that's difficult to do with an infant. I tried to reason with him—I suggested we move closer to my mother so she can help with some of the care-giving responsibilities, but he won't have it. He said that I should be able to manage everything, that I should just "get it together." He makes comments that I am a disappointment as a wife and mother. I'm trying my best, and it's hurtful to hear the man I love make statements like that. He's banned my friends from coming over to the house recently. He said that they're distracting me from my responsibilities. Really, they were my saving grace. Lately, I feel like I don't even know the man I married. This is definitely not what I had in mind when we were going to start our family, and I want desperately for things to be the way they used to be. His actions make me think twice about how honest he was when he told me about his previous marriage. Maybe she did not have anger management problems. I'm starting to wonder if he was the one who was abusive and not her—maybe there was no such thing as self-defense after all.

Examples of characteristics of abusive men: Write the characteristic displayed and back it up with examples from the vignette:

1.

2.

3.

Answer Key:

Vignette #1:

1. Pushes for quick involvement/ Pressures for commitment too quickly
2. Blames others for his problems or mistakes
3. Hypersensitivity
4. Verbally abusive

Vignette #2:

1. Unrealistic expectations
2. Isolation
3. Verbally abusive
4. Rigid sex roles
5. Past battering

EA 3: PERPETRATOR TRUE/FALSE

Into the Mind of a DV Perpetrator Quiz

Write True or False in the space provided

1. The abuser may demonstrate extreme jealousy with your attachment with your friends and family_____

2. The abuser never try to control you or any aspect of your life_____

3. An abuser may pressure you for an exclusive commitment right away and claim that he has never felt that way with anyone else_____

4. An abuser always takes responsibility and never shifts the responsibility onto others for his actions._____

5. An abuser would never attempt to isolate you from your family and friends_____

6. An abuser would never blame the victim for how he feels. He never feels that his feelings are caused by others._____

7. An abuser can seem understanding one minute, and then suddenly switch to being angry and distant the next DV_____

8. An abuser would never say that the victim deserved the abuse._____

9. IOA 1: ABUSE AND FAMILY DYNAMICS

ABUSIVE MEN AND FAMILY DYNAMICS

1. **Promoting disrespect for the mother and her parental authority**

Effects of violence, verbal abuse, and victim blaming	Children may identify with the abuser and begin see their mother as pathetic, helpless, stupid, incompetent, weak, unworthy of respect, and some will even see her as a legitimate target of the abuse perpetrated against her.
Calculated Strategies	Abuser disrupts the mother's attempts to create structure and stability; contradicts her rules; reinforces and rewards child's disrespectful behavior toward the mother.
After separation	Abuser may alienate child from mother; may seek custody as vengeance.

2. **Negatively influencing the mother /child relationship**

Direct impact	Abuser may prevent mother from comforting distressed child; may force children to watch distressed mother during abuse.
Indirect impact	Abuse promotes a variety of problems including depression, anxiety, poor sleeping, rage, PTSD, loss of confidence so mother cannot focus on the needs of children; may increase likelihood of maltreatment, use of drugs/alcohol, or permissive and parental neglect.

Children's disengaging from mother	More pronounced in boys and teenagers of either sex, the development of identification with the abuser and contempt for the mother or being ashamed to be associated with her.
Violence by children against mother	Also more common in boys, and most often after a separation, a child takes on the role of perpetrator, sometimes to win the approval of the absent abuser.
3. Using the child as a means to perpetrate abuse	
During relationship	Abuser maltreats, neglects, or perpetrates other behavior harmful to child (e.g., destroying personal property to hurt mother; having child spy on mother; deliberate endangering child; threatening to harm, kidnap or kill child; leaving the family destitute; or reporting the mother to DCFS).
After relationship	Abuser blames mother for separation; enlists child's support to pressure mother for reconciliation; uses child to communicate with or spy on mother; seeks custody.
4. Impact on the family system	
Chronic fear and emotional deprivation	Unhealthy, dysfunctional dynamics become solidified among family members; children may compete for abuser's attention because his attention and affection are scarce.
Role reversal	Parentification of children (i.e., adopting or being given a parental role in the family) and infantilizing of mother (i.e., treating her like a child) may over time see the woman being protected by child; child may try to predict and prevent violence by the abuser.

Adapted from *The Batterer as Parent (2002)* by Lundy Bancroft & Jay Silverman.

IOA 4: RED FLAGS CHECKLIST

Red Flags in Relationships

Psychologist Lundy Bancroft has compiled a list of warning signs that help aid women in early detection of potential abuse down the road early in ones relationship in his book entitled *Why Does He Do That? Inside the Minds of Angry and Controlling Men.* Below is a listing of several red flag indicators revealed in the book.

1. He speaks disrespectfully about former partners

It is very common for people to have difficult feelings after ending a relationship but pay particular attention if his anger toward the previous partner is s not uncommon for people to have hard feelings after a break-up but be careful if his anger toward a previous partner (or partners) is unusually resentful and you notice any of these things:
- The abuser uses insults and degrading language to describe a former partner.
- He assumes the role of a victim of abuse by her.
- He claims she wrongly accused him of abuse.
- He blames all problems in their relationship on her and accepts no responsibility
- He admits he abused a past partner but justifies his abuse with an excuse (e.g., drinking, former abuse history, or stating she caused the abuse.)
- He praises you for being better than she was.
- He claims you are the only woman who really understands him.

How do you think and feel in response?
- You feel sympathetic toward him because of how badly his ex-partner treated or treats him.
- You compete to be a good partner and better than she was .

2. He treats you in a disrespectful manner

You may be ideal at first, but he eventually finds fault with nearly everything you say and do.
- He insults you, puts you down, criticizes, and ridicules you.
- He doesn't respect your opinions, discounts you.
- He humiliates you in front of other people and in private.
- He compares you to previous partners and says you are not as good as they were.
- He blames you for things he himself does wrong.
- He criticizes you if you dispute against disrespectful treatment.

3. He makes you uncomfortable by doing favours or being generous

This sounds great at first, but pay attention to your level of discomfort.
- He insists on doing favors for you no matter how much you protest.

- He claims you owe him favourable treatment because of his favours to you.
- He brings up his past favours and makes you feel guilty if you do something he disapproves of.

4. He is controlling and possessive

This starts subtly and can initially be mistaken for his intense interest in you. These are some ways control can look early in a relationship:
- He has activities all planned out for your dates.
- He is not interested in hearing your ideas for activities or contributions to planning them.
- He has strong opinions on how you should dress and look.
- He pressures you to spend all your time with him.
- He gives you advice you didn't ask for.

Adapted from from: *Helping Abused Women in Shelters: 101 Things to Know, Say & Do* (Cunningham & Baker 2008)

Red Flags In Relationships: Worksheet 1

Vignette #1: Kiani

I was in a domestic violence relationship for a year with the man who I thought was my soul mate. It was difficult to leave, but with the help of my mother, I was able to get out and get a restraining order to keep me safe. That was 3 years ago. Fast forward to 1 month ago….I started dating again. I was scared to end up in the same situation again but I felt more confident this time. Never again would I be hurt like that. I met Chris through an online dating website. After meeting 2 guys before him and not feeling a connection, I was skeptical but changed my mind after our first date. Chris planned everything for our date—a romantic restaurant and a walk on the pier. He planned our next several dates in order to surprise me. He would tell me how to dress for the date, so I was prepared. The dates were always fun, and I thought it was sweet that he took time out for me like that. Our relationship progressed fast, and before I knew it, I was spending all of my time with Chris. Whenever he was not at work or with friends, he was with me. He called me on his breaks at work to see how I was doing and said he couldn't wait to see me again. He started planning vacations together months in advance, because he knew that this was going to be a long-term relationship a month into it. I thought it was too soon for that, but then again, things were going great. While at his house one evening, Chris talked to me about his family. He talked about how his dad provided for the family while his mom took care of the children and the house. Chris said that it was the men's responsibility to take care of the weaker sex—after all they got higher paying jobs. I'm working to become an accountant and shared my opinion on how society has changed and that women can do a lot more than he's giving them credit for. He became upset and said that my opinion was invalid. He raised his voice and made a comment how none of his past girlfriends would ever be stupid enough to say something like that

What red flags are present in Kiani's relationship with Chris? Write what you see and back it up with examples from the vignette:

1. _____
_____
_____

2. _____
_____
_____

3. _____
_____
_____

Vignette #2: Autumn

Will and I met through one of my mother's coworkers. We haven't been dating long, only 3 months, but I enjoy our time together, and I think he may be the one. I know it's too soon to tell, but he makes me feel special. He always pays for everything—whenever I ask to help out, he insists that he pays. He says it's his way of letting me know how much he cares for me. After a month of dating, we were alone at his place and started kissing intensely. One thing lead to another, and Will was asking to have sex. It was too soon for me, and I let him know, but he wouldn't let it go. He said we both felt like things were going well. He said he has done a lot for me that he would've never done for past girlfriends, like the time he came to change my flat tire early in the morning so I could make it to work on time. He was right, it felt like we had known each other much longer, so I gave in to the moment. Will told me how thankful he was for meeting me because his last relationship was a nightmare. He told me about how she used to put him down and how she used to destroy things in the house during arguments. One time, she even called the police on him, claiming domestic violence. Will said I was nothing like her….I was smart, creative and beautiful. Those were all characteristics he admired. I felt bad for him because he was a caring and generous man. He worked hard to meet his goals, and he, of all people, didn't deserve to be treated like that. The only problem that Will had was that he was struggling to stop using prescription pain pills. The pills were prescribed to him after his knee surgery 8 months ago. He admits that sometimes he continues using the pills to prevent withdrawal symptoms. I expressed my concerns and told him he needs to seek help, but he dismissed my advice and said he could do it on his own.

What red flags are present in Autumn's relationship with Will? Write what you see and back it up with examples from the vignette:

1. _____
_____
_____
_____

2. _____
_____
_____
_____

3. _____
_____
_____
_____

Vignette #3: Karla Part 1

Mike and I met through an online dating website. We've only been dating for a week, but it feels like it's already grown into a serious relationship. That probably just means this relationship is really meant to be. Our first date was amazing! It was so refreshing to finally be going on a date after being single for so long. I remember being so excited that I went out and bought a brand new outfit, with accessories and all, just for this date. I went and had my hair professionally done into a cute bun, and I had my make up done. I wanted this date to be perfect. I must say—I was a little disappointed when Mike insisted that I specifically wear a red mini skirt and a tube top that he bought for me for our first date. He had special plans for the date, and told me how important it was for me to wear that specific dress. That was a little strange to me, but I did appreciate the fact that he bought me a brand new dress. So he told me to be ready by 6 pm on Friday night, and offered to pick me up. I felt more comfortable driving to meet him at the spot, since this was a first date, and I really didn't know him all that well. Funny thing happened—his offer sort of turned into a demand, as he insisted on picking me up. Mike believed that it wouldn't be romantic if he didn't pick me up. That made a little sense to me. It was annoying, but not a big deal, so I acquiesced, although, in my mind I was thinking that this would probably be the first and the last date with Mike. Fast-forward to Friday night, Mike arrives early with roses in one hand and my red dress in the other. I felt so special at that moment! I hurriedly put on the red dress, and left to embark on this mystery date. After half an hour of driving, we get to this fancy restraint. The waitress comes to take my order, and Mike orders for me. I was shocked. I wanted to say something, but…it wasn't like I'm paying for my food. So, I just smiled and sat there, even though I was incredibly uncomfortable with this. When my order arrived, it was pretty good, so I wasn't as bothered. The date went fairly well overall, except for when Mike would make comments about my hair and makeup. That really bothered me, because I had done my hair and makeup specifically for this date! He would tell me that he likes my hair down and literally had the nerve to tell me to take the bun down. He said the bun makes me look old. I was a little upset, but when I took it down he groveled about how beautiful I was. He would tell me how well my hair frames my face and brings out my eyes. He sure knew how to make me feel special after making me feel bad. He's not that bad, but I don't know about a second date.

What red flags are present in Karla's relationship with Mike? Write what you see and back it up with examples from the vignette:

1. _____
_____
_____
_____

2. _____
_____
_____
_____

3. _____
_____
_____

Vignette #4 Karla Part 2

I actually never intended to go on a second date with Mike. But, to my surprise, during the end of our first date, Mike had already planned the second date. Again, he insisted on picking me up sometime in the evening the next day. He picked me up on time, but this time, instead of buying me an outfit, he told me to dress casual. He also insisted that I wear my hair down. I felt really uncomfortable with being told what to wear, but figured there might be a good reason. Anyway, we had lunch at a nice restaurant, and after that we went hiking. Mike kept complementing me on my fun and carefree personality and comparing me to his ex-girlfriend. He told me that his ex-girlfriend was never fun to be around and that she was stupid and made it difficult for him to be the man of the relationship. I wondered what he meant by that. He continued to say that his ex-girlfriend was stupid to think women were equal to men. Mike went on and on about how we are such a perfect couple. I didn't even know we were a couple yet! Nothing ever moved this fast with me, I was having a hard time keeping up.

What red flags are present in Karla's relationship with Mike? Write what you see and back it up with examples from the vignette:

1. _____
_____
_____
_____

2. _____
_____
_____
_____

3. _____
_____
_____
_____

IOA 4: RED FLAGS ANSWER KEY

Answer Key:

Vignette #1:

1. He's controlling
    a. Has activities planned for all dates
    b. Has opinions on how she should dress

2. He's possessive
    a. Calls several times a day to check-in
    b. Wants to spend every minute with her, when it's convenient for him

3. Gets serious too quickly
    a. Planning vacations a month into dating

4. Has negative attitudes about women
    a. They're the weaker sex
    b. Men take care of them
    c. Women are caretakers, get paid less

5. He's disrespectful
    a. Insults and puts down
    b. Doesn't respect opinions
    c. Compares to previous partners

Vignette #2:
1. Makes her uncomfortable by doing favors or being generous
    a. Insists on doing something (paying for everything)
    b. Brings up past favors (changing flat tire) and makes her feel guilty

2. Pressures for sex

3. Speaks disrespectfully about former partners
    a. Started soon after meeting
    b. Claims she falsely accused of abuse
    c. Paints himself as a victim
    d. Praises for being better than she was
    e. Expects her to feel sorry for him because of how badly he was treated

4. Abuses drugs or alcohol

Vignette #3 Part 1 and Part 2
1. Makes her uncomfortable by doing favors or being generous
   a. Insists on doing something (paying for everything, picking her up from home, buying her dress)

2. Disrespectful
   a. Insults, puts down
   b. Compares to previous partners

3. Controlling
   a. Has activities planned, tells her what to wear and how to style her hair
   b. Insists on picking her up

IOA 5: SELF-DEFEATING THOUGHTS

What Are Your Self-Defeating Thoughts?

Name:

What is a negative or self-defeating thought that brings you down?:

How can you change that thought to make it positive and self-motivating?:

Draw a depiction of how the negative or self-defeating thought makes you feel and how the positive or self-motivating thought makes you feel. It may be a literal drawing of the emotion or a creative representation how you feel.

C1: FINAL EXAM

DV only involves physical abuse.	True	False
The Power and Control Wheel includes physical and emotional abuse, but does not include sexual and economic abuse.	True	False
DV is centered on a person's abusive use of power to control another.	True	False
An abuser always takes responsibility for his actions and never shifts the responsibility to his victim.	True	False
Research identifies DV as the number one health issue among African American women.	True	False
An abuser would never attempt to isolate his victims from her friends and family.	True	False
An abuser would never blame his victim for how he feels. He never feels that his feelings are cause by others.	True	False
An abuser can seem understanding one minute and then suddenly switch to being angry and distant the next.	True	False
Entitlement is identified as the "overarching attitudinal characteristic" of abusive men.	True	False
Children who witness domestic violence in their homes are largely unaffected.	True	False
The abuser would never say that the victim deserves her abuse.	True	False

1. Identify five types of abuse that are included in the Power and Control Wheel:

   _____
   _____
   _____
   _____
   _____

2. Give an example of each of the five types of abuse:

   _____
   _____
   _____
   _____
   _____
   _____
   _____

3. There are three phases in the Cycle of Violence that shows how domestic violence involves a cyclical set of behaviors. Those three phases are: Tension Building Phase, Explosion Phase, and Honeymoon Phase.
   Provide a description of each phase:

   _____
   _____
   _____
   _____
   _____
   _____

4. Write out one positive affirmation that appeals to you. (You can come up with one on your own or write one that you have heard before.):

   _____
   _____
   _____

5. List four components of the Equality Wheel:

   _____
   _____
   _____
   _____
   _____
   _____

What are four qualities in a healthy relationship?:

_____
_____
_____
_____
_____

6. List five safety planning strategies:

_____
_____
_____
_____
_____
_____

C2: GET TO KNOW YOU

How Well Do You Know Me?

Choose a partner with whom you would like to engage in a conversation. Discuss with your partner the nine items below. Listen carefully to your partner's answers and be prepared to present what your partner has discussed with you. You may list your partner's interview answers on a sheet of paper to guide your presentation.

1. Identify your name and where you're from.

2. What's your favorite color, type of food, and hobby?

3. What have you learned so far from the groups you've attended?

4. What DV information do you find the most applicable to your life?

5. If you're life could be exactly as you want it to be, what would it look like? What would you be doing and where would you be? How would your ideal like look?

6. If you could travel anywhere, where would you go?

7. What are two things you love about yourself?

8. What is one thing you would like to improve about yourself?

9. Identify two things that make you feel better when you're feeling down?

10. Identify one thing you like about your activity partner?

C2: GET TO KNOW YOU

1. _____
2. _____
3. _____
4. _____
5. _____
6. _____
7. _____
8. _____
9. _____
10. _____
11. _____
12. _____
13. _____
14. _____
15. _____
16. _____
17. _____
18. _____
19. _____
20. _____

C3: Affirmations

Scriptural Affirmations

1. I will follow after the things which bring peace, and things wherewith I may edify another. (Romans 14:19)

2. I choose to forgive, even as God for Christ's sake has forgiven me. (Ephesians 4:32)

3. I did not receive the spirit of slavery to fall back into fear, but I have received the Spirit. (Romans 8:15)

4. For God did not give me the spirit of fear and timidity, but of power, love and self-discipline (2 Timothy 1:7)

5. The Lord is my Helper- I will not fear: what can man do to me? (Hebrews 13:6)

6. I will not throw away my confidence, which has a great reward. (Hebrews 10:35-36)

7. In all my ways, I will acknowledge the Lord and He will make straight my paths. (Proverbs 3:6)

8. There is no fear in love, but perfect love casts out fear. (1 John 4:18)

9. He said to me, "My grace is sufficient for you, for my power is made perfect in weakness." (2nd Corinthians 12:19)

10. I will fear not, for HE is with me. I will not be dismayed, for He is my God and my God will strengthen me, help me and uphold me with HIS righteous right hand. (Isaiah 41:10)

11. Love is patient and kind, love does not envy or boast; it is not arrogant or rude. It doesn't insist on its own way; It is not irritable or resentful; It doesn't rejoice in wrongdoing, but rejoices with the truth. Love bears all things, believes all things, hopes all things, endures all things. (1 Corinthians 13: 4-7)

12. O Lord, you hear the desire of the afflicted, you will strengthen my heart, and You will incline your eat to do justice to the fatherless and the oppressed, so that the man who is of the earth may strike terror no more. (Psalm 10:17-18)

13. Today I am be slow to speak, quick to hear, slow to anger. (James 1:19-20)

14. Not by might, not by power, but by My Spirit saith the Lord of Hosts. (Zechariah 4:6)

15. I can do all things through Christ who strengthens me. (Philippians 4:13)

16. I praise you—for I am fearfully and wonderfully made. (Psalm 139:14)

17. For everyone who calls on the name of the Lord will be saved. (Romans 10:13)

18. I am developing my Spiritual gifts each day. (I Corinthians 12:28)

19. Today I let go of useless anger. (Proverbs 29:11)

20. Today I will focus on the present moment. (Isaiah 30:15)

21. I seek positive experiences. (Psalm 8:3)

22. I cast my cares upon Jesus, as he gives me rest. (Matthew 11:28)

23. Today I speak out strongly what I have to say. (Exodus 7:2)

24. Today I confidently approach tough situations. (Hebrews 4:16)

25. I find meaning and purpose in Jesus. (Romans 8:28)

26. I encourage myself while encouraging others. (Hebrews 10:28)

27. God's grace is sufficient for me. (2 Corinthians 12:9)

28. All things are possible through Christ who strengthens me. (Luke 18:27)

29. The Lord will direct my path. (Proverbs 3: 5-6)

30. God will supply all my needs. (Philippians 4:19)

31. God will never leave me (Hebrews 13:5)

C3: Affirmations

Positive Affirmations

1. I treat myself with kindness.

2. I am a worthwhile person.

3. I set appropriate boundaries and enforce them.

4. I respect other people's boundaries.

5. With my Higher Power's help, my direction in life is clear.

6. I release my fear of truly feeling my feelings.

7. Today, I am willing.

8. I observe the good things that happen in my life.

9. There is a lot to be happy for—God has a plan for me.

10. I am perfectly me.

11. I celebrate all my successes, large and small.

12. I trust myself.

13. As I turn negatives into positives, my life changes for the better.

14. I am loving—I am loved—I am lovable.

15. I keep improving.

16. I am healing.

17. Today, I have whatever I need.

18. I open myself to receive love—and to love others.

19. I am enough.

20. I am enough, and I have enough.

21. Today, and every day, I allow myself to be me.

22. I am all right; I am OK; I am successful in whatever I do.

23. I am grateful for all that I am.

24. I can never fail at being me.

25. I can handle it, whatever it is.

26. I respect myself and act in accordance with my own values.

27. I am capable of change.

28. I make amends when appropriate.

29. I matter.

30. I forgive others and myself.

31. I am changing.

32. I am worth listening to.

33. I trust my emotions and my thoughts.

34. I feel. I share. I trust.

35. I can feel my emotions without being overwhelmed by my emotions.

36. I am grateful for my friends.

37. I am comfortable with myself.

38. I am comfortable with others and myself.

39. I am able to say "no."

40. I express my anger appropriately.

41. I am uniquely me, and I share my humanity with all.

42. I am honest and direct.

43. I like myself and accept myself as I am.

44. I am on a wonderful journey of healing.

45. I have choices in life.

46. I take care of myself physically and emotionally.

47. I love and I am loved, by myself and by my God.

48. I am capable human being.

49. I am a skillful and artistic person.

50. Nothing is worth losing my sanity over.

51. I am responsible for my own feelings.

52. I have the right to feel the way I do.

53. I am able to handle the problems I face with the help of my God

For God has not given us a spirit of fear and timidity, but of power, love, and self-discipline.
2 Timothy 1:7

References & Further Readings

American Psychiatric Association (APA). (2000). *Diagnostic and statistical manual of mental disorders* (4th ed., text rev.). Washington, DC: Author.

Anderson, N.C., & Black, D.W. (1995). Introductory textbook of psychiatry (2nd ed.). Washington, DC: American Psychiatric Press.

Astin, M.C., Lawrence, K.J., & Foy, D.W. (1993). Posttraumatic stress disorder among battered women: Risk and resiliency factors. Violence *and Victims, 8*, 17-28.

Basile, K. C., Arias, I., Desai, S., & Thompson, M. P. (2004). The differential association of intimate partner physical, sexual, psychological, and stalking violence and posttraumatic stress symptoms in a nationally representative sample of women. *Journal of Traumatic Stress, 17*(5), 413-421. http://dx.doi.org/10.1023/B:JOTS.0000048954.50232.d8

Bent-Goodley, T. B. (2001). Eradicating domestic violence in the African American community: A literature review and action agenda. *Journal of Violence, Trauma, and Abuse, 2*, 316-330. http://dx.doi.org/10.1177/1524838001002004003

Bent-Goodley, T. B. (2004). Perceptions of domestic violence: A dialogue with African American women. *Health and Social Work, 29*(4), 307-316. http://dx.doi.org/10.1093/hsw/29.4.307

Bent-Goodley, T. B. (2005). An African-centered approach to domestic violence. *Families in Society, 86*(2), 197-206. http://dx.doi.org/10.1606/1044-3894.2455

Bent-Goodley, T. B. (2007). Health disparities and violence against women: Why and how cultural and societal influences matter. *Trauma, Violence, & Abuse, 8*(2), 90-104. http://dx.doi.org/10.1177/1524838007301160

Bent-Goodley, T. B., & Fowler, D. N. (2006). Spiritual and religious abuse: Expanding what is known about domestic violence. *Journal of Women and Social Work, 21*(4), 282-285. http://dx.doi.org/10.1177/0886109906288901

Bureau of Justice Statistics (2001) *National Crime Victimization Survey*. U.S. Department of Justice

Billingsley, A. (1992). *Climbing Jacob's ladder: The enduring legacy of African American families*. New York, NY: Simon.

Black, M. C., Basile, K. C., Breiding, M. J., Smith, S. G., Walters, M. L., Merrick, M. T., Chen, J., & Stevens, M. R. (2011). *The National Intimate Partner and Sexual Violence Survey (NISVS): 2010 summary report*. Atlanta, GA: National Center for Injury Prevention and Control, Centers for Disease Control and Prevention.

Campbell, J. C., & Belknap, R.A. (1997). Predictors of depression in battered women. *Violence Against Women, 3*(3), 271-294. http://dx.doi.org/10.1177/1077801297003003004

Campbell, D., Sharps, P., Gary, F., Campbell, J., Lopez, L., (January 31, 2002). "Intimate Partner Violence in African American Women". *Online Journal of Issues in Nursing*. Vol. 7 No. 1, Manuscript 4. http://www.nursingworld.org/MainMenuCategories/ANAMarketplace/ANAPeriodicals/OJIN/TableofContents/Volume72002/No1Jan2002/AfricanAmericanWomenPartnerViolence.aspx

Campbell, J. C., & Soeken, K. L. (1999). Women's responses to battering over time: An analysis of change. *Journal of Personality and Social Psychology, 56*(2), 267-283.

Campbell, J. C., & Wolf, A. D. (2006). The realities and health disparities of domestic violence for women of color [Webcast]. Paper presented at the Health Resources and Services Administration web conference. Retrieved from http://webcast.hrsa.gov/archives/mchb/dhsps/october2006/DHSPS101006slides.pdf

Coker, A. L., Smith, P. H., Thompson, M. P., McKeown, R. E., Bethea, L., & Davis, K. E. (2002). Social support protects against the negative effects of partner violence on mental health. *Journal of Women's Health and Gender-Based Medicine, 11*(5), 465-475. http://dx.doi.org/10.1089/15246090260137644

Connor, K.M., Davidson, J.R.T., & Lee, L. c. (2003). Spirituality, resilience and anger in survivors of violent trauma: A community survey. *Journal of Traumatic Stress, 16,* 487-494.

El-Khoury, M., Dutton, M.A., Goodman, L., Engel, L., Belamaric, R., Murphy, M. & Somberg, R. (2004). Ethnic differences in battered women's help-seeking strategies: A focus on mental health and spirituality. Cultural Diversity and Ethnic Minority Psychology, Vol. 10, No. 4, 383–393.

Ellison, C.G., & Anderson, K.L. (2001). Religious involvement and domestic violence among U.S. couples. *Journal for the Scientific Study of Religion, 40,* 269—286.

Ellison, C. G., Trinitapoli, J. A., Anderson, K. L., & Johnson, B. R. (2007). Race, religious involvement, and domestic violence. *Violence Against Women, 13*(11), 1094-1100. http://dx.doi.org/10.1177/1077801207308259

Fagan, J. (1996). *The criminalization of domestic violence: Promises and limits.* Washington, DC: U.S. Department of Justice.

Fraser, I. M., McNutt, L., Clark, C., Williams-Muhammed, D., & Lee, R. (2002). Social support choices for help with abusive re lationships: Perceptions of African American women. *Journal of Family Violence, 17*(4), 363-375. http://dx.doi.org/10.1023/A:1020322600490

Giblin, M. J. (1999). Catholic Church teaching and domestic violence. *Listening: Journal of Religion and Culture, 34*, 10-21.

Gilbert, M. C. (2000). Spirituality in social work groups: Practitioners speak out. *Social Work With Groups, 22*(4), 67-84. http://dx.doi.org/10.1300/J009v22n04_06

Gillum, T., Sullivan, C. M., & Bybee, D. I. (2006). The importance of spirituality in the lives of domestic violence survivors. *Violence Against Women, 12*(3), 240-250. http://dx.doi.org/10.1177/1077801206286224

Gleason, W. J. (1993). Mental disorders in battered women: An empirical study. *Violence and Victim, 8*(1), 53-68.

Goldberg, W. G., & Tomlanovich, M. C. (1984). Domestic violence victims in the emergency department. *Journal of the American Medical Association, 251*, 3259-3264. http://dx.doi.org/10.1001/jama.1984.03340480041025

Grovert, A. (2008). *Domestic violence against women: A literature review* (Unpublished master's thesis). Pacific University, Oregon. Retrieved from http://commons.pacificu.edu/cgi/viewcontent.cgi?article=1037&context=spp

Hampton, R., Oliver, W., & Magarian, L. (2003). Domestic violence in the African American community: An analysis of social and structural factors. *Violence Against Women, 9*(5), 533-537. http://dx.doi.org/10.1177/1077801202250450

Hampton, R. L., Gelles, R.J., & Harrop, J. C. (1989). Is violence in Black families increasing? A comparison of 1975 and 1985 national survey rates. *Journal of Marriage and Family, 51*, 969-980.

Hampton, R. L., LaTaillade, J. J., Dacey, A., & Marghi, J. R. (2008). Evaluating domestic violence interventions for black women. *Journal of Aggression,*

Maltreatment, and Trauma, 16(3), 330-353. http://dx.doi.org/10.1007/s10896-011-9358-4

Hill, H. M., Hawkins, S. R., Raposa, M., & Carr, P. (1995). Relationship between multiple exposures to violence and coping strategies among African American mothers. *Violence and Victims, 10*, 55-71.

Hooks, B. (2003). Rock my soul: Black people and self-esteem. New York: Atria

Hughes, M. J., & Rasmussen, L. A. (2010). The utility of motivational interviewing in domestic violence shelters: A qualitative exploration. *Journal of Aggression, Maltreatment and Trauma, 19*(3), 300-322. http://dx.doi.org/10.1080/10926771003705213

Krause, N. (2004). Common facets of religion, unique facets of religion, and life satisfaction among older African Americans. *Journal of Gerontology: Social Sciences, 58*, S160-S170.

Kupenda, A. M. (1998, Fall). Law, life, and literature: A critical reflection of life and literature to illuminate how laws of domestic violence, race, and class bind Black women based on Alice Walker's book *The Third Life of Grange Copeland*. *Howard Law Journal, 42*, 1-26.

Lacey, K. K., McPherson, M. D., Samuel, P. S., Sears, K. P., & Head, D. (2012). The impact of different types of intimate partner violence on the mental and physical health of women in different ethnic groups. *Journal of Interpersonal Violence, 28*(2), 359-385. http://dx.doi.org/10.1177/0886260512454743

Lee, R.K., Thompson, V.L., & Mechanic, M.B. (2002) Intimate partner violence and women of color: A call for innovations. *American Journal of Public Health, 92*, 530-534.

Lincoln, C. E., & Mamiya, L. H. (1990). *The Black church in the African American experience.* Durham, NC: Duke University Press.

Manetta, A. A., Bryant, D. F., Cavanaugh, T., & Gange, T. A. (2003). The church—Does it provide support for abused women? Differences in the perceptions of battered women and parishioners. *Journal of Religion and Abuse, 5*(1), 5-21. http://dx.doi.org/10.1300/J154v05n01_02

Martin, E. P., & Martin, J. M. (2002). *Spirituality and the Black helping tradition in social work.* Washington, DC: NASW Press.

Matthews, D. D. (2004). *Domestic violence sourcebook* (2nd ed.). Detroit, MI: Omnigraphics.

Mattis, J. S. (2002). Religion and spirituality in the meaning-making and coping experiences of African American women: A qualitative analysis. Psychology of Women Quarterly, 26, 309-321, doi.org/10.1111/1471-6402.t01-2-00070.

Moore, T. (1991). The African American church: A source of empowerment, mutual help, and social change. *Prevention in Human Services, 10,* 147-167. http://dx.doi.org/10.1300/J293v10n01_09

National Association of Social Workers. (2000). Cultural competence in the social work profession. In *Social work speaks: NASW policy statements* (pp. 59-62). Washington, DC: NASW Press.

Nason-Clark, N. (1997). The battered wife: How Christians confront family violence. Louisville, KY: Westminster.John Knox Press.

Nason-Clark, N. (2000). Making the sacred safe: Women and abuse and communities of faith. Presidential address. *Sociology of Religion, 61,* 349-368.

Paranjape, A., & Kaslow, N. (2010). Family violence exposure and health outcomes among older African American women: Do spirituality and social support play protective roles? *Journal of Women's Health, 19*(10), 1899-1904. http://dx.doi.org/10.1089/jwh.2009.1845

Potter, H. (2007). Battered black women's use of religious services and spirituality for assistance in leaving abusive relationships. *Violence Against Women, 13*, 262. http://dx.doi.org/10.1177/1077801206297438

Rasmussen, L. A., Hughes, M. J., & Murray, C. A. (2008) Applying motivational interviewing in a domestic violence shelter: A pilot study evaluating the training of shelter staff. *Journal of Aggression, Maltreatment, and Trauma, 17*(3), 300-322. http://dx.doi.org/10.1080/10926770802402980

Rennison, C. M., & Welchans, S. (2000, May). *Intimate partner violence*. Washington, DC: U.S. Department of Justice, Bureau of Justice Statistics.

Schechter, S., & Ganley, A. L. (1995). *Domestic violence: A national curriculum for family preservation practitioners.* San Francisco, CA: Family Violence Prevention Fund.

Smith, P. R. (2009). Resilience: Resistance factor for depressive symptom. *Journal of Psychiatric and Mental Health Nursing, 16*(9), 829-837. http://dx.doi.org/10.1111/j.1365-2850.2009.01463.x

Straus, M. A., Gelles, R. J., & Steinmetz, S. K. (1980). *Behind closed doors. Violence in the American family.* Garden City, NY: Doubleday.

Taylor, R. J., Chatters, L. M., & Levin, J. S. (2004). *Religion in the lives of African Americans.* Thousand Oaks, CA; Sage.

Taylor, R. J., Ellison, L. M., Chatters, L. M., Levin, J. S., & Lincoln, K. D. (2000). Mental health services in faith communities: The role of clergy in black churches. *Social Work*, 45, 73-87. http://dx.doi.org/10.1093/sw/45.1.73

Thomas, M., & Holmes, B. (1992). Determinants of satisfaction for Blacks and Whites. *Sociological Quarterly, 33,* 459-472.

Thompson, V.S., & Basile, A. (2000). *African American Attitudes toward Domestic Violence and DV Assistance.* http://www.musc.edu/vawprevention/index.html

Tjaden, P., & Thoennes, N. (2000). *Extent, nature and consequences of intimate partner violence: Findings from the National Violence Against Women Survey.* Washington, DC: United States Department of Justice, Office of Justice Program.

Vitanza, S., Vogel, L.C., M, & Marshall, L.L. (1995). Distress and symptoms of posttraumatic stress disorder in abused women. Violence and Victims, 10(1), 23-34.

Walker, L. (1998). Lifting the "political gag order": Breaking the silence around partner violence in ethnic minority families. In J. L. Jasinski & L. M. Williams (Eds.), *Partner violence: A comprehensive review of 20 years of research* (pp. 184-209). Thousand Oaks, CA; Sage.

Wang, M., Horne, S. G., Levitt, H. M., & Klesges, L. M. (2009). Christian women in IPV relationships: An exploratory study of religious factors. *Journal of Psychology and Christianity, 28*(3), 224-235. http://dx.doi.org/10.1186/1472-6874-8-4

Watlington, C. G., & Murphy, C. M. (2006). The roles of religion and spirituality among African American survivors of domestic violence. *Journal of Clinical Psychology, 62*(7), 837-857. http://dx.doi.org/10.1002/jclp.20268

Websdale, N. (1999). *Understanding domestic homicide*. Boston, MA: Northeastern University Press.

West, T. C. (1999). *Wounds of the spirit: Black women, violence, and resistance ethics.* New York, NY: New York University Press.

Wilson, M., & Daly, M. (1992). Till death do us part. In J. Radford & D. E. H. Russell (Eds.), *Femicide: The politics of woman killing* (pp. 83-93). Boston, MA: Twayne.

Woods, T.E., Antoni, M.H., Ironson, G.H. & Kling, D.W. (1999). Religiosity is associated with affective and immune status in symnptomatic HIV-infected gay men. *Journal of Psychosomatic Research, 46*, 165-176.

Resources

2-1-1 Information and Referral Search
www.211us.org

National Coalition against Domestic Violence
Anonymous and Confidential Hotline 24/7:
1.800.799.SAFE (7233)
1.800.787.3224 (TTY
http://www.ncadv.org/

Institute on Domestic Violence in the African American Community
St Paul, MN 55108
Phone: (612) 624-5357
Fax: (612) 624-9201
www.dvinstitute.org

Sacred Circle
Rapid City, SD 57701
Phone: (605) 341-2472
Fax: (605) 341-2472
www.sacred-circle.com

The Black Church and Domestic Violence Institute
Atlanta, GA 30331
Phone: (770) 909-0715
Fax: (770) 907-4069
www.bcdvi.org

Faith Trust Institute
Seattle, WA 98103
Phone: (206) 634-1903
Fax (206) 634-0115
www.faithtrustinstitute.org

Women of Color Network
6400 Flank Drive, Suite 1300
Harrisburg, PA 17112
800 537-2238
http://womenofcolornetwork.org/

American Association of Christian Counseling
Multicultural Division of American Association of Christian Counselors
http://mcd.aacc.net/

Presbyterian Against Domestic Violence Network
1(800)872-3283
http://www.pcusa.org

Recovery Books for Children Exposed to Family Violence

A Place for Starr: A Story of Hope for Children Experiencing Family Violence
By: Howard Schor
Kidsright; (2002)
ISBN: 1558640827

A Terrible Thing Happened- A story for children who have witness violence or trauma
By: Margaret M. Holmes, Sasha J. Mudlaff, Cary Pillo
Magination Press; (January 1, 2000)
ISBN: 1557987017

A Safe Place to Live: A story for Children Who Have Experienced Domestic Violence
By: Michelle A. Harrison, Luanne Marten
Kidsright (January 2001)
ISBN: 1558640908

Something Is Wrong at My House
By: Diane Davis
Parenting Press; (December, 1984)
ISBD: 0943990106

Talking about Domestic Violence
By: Nicholas Edwards
Chrysalis Education; (October 2003)
ISBD: 1932333088

www.ingramcontent.com/pod-product-compliance
Lightning Source LLC
Chambersburg PA
CBHW081156290426
44108CB00018B/2568